Legends of the Wrestling Ring

MD Sharr

Published by pinky, 2024.

While every precaution has been taken in the preparation of this book, the publisher assumes no responsibility for errors or omissions, or for damages resulting from the use of the information contained herein.

LEGENDS OF THE WRESTLING RING

First edition. November 20, 2024.

Copyright © 2024 MD Sharr.

ISBN: 979-8230325710

Written by MD Sharr.

Table of Contents

Preface 1
1. Steve Austin: The Journey of a Wrestling Legend 4
2. Dwayne Johnson: A Legend Beyond the Ring........................ 7
3. Hulk Hogan: The Immortal Icon of Wrestling 10
4. John Cena: The Face That Runs the Place 13
5. The Undertaker: The Phenom of Wrestling 16
6. Shawn Michaels: The Showstopper of Wrestling 19
7. Bret Hart: The Excellence of Execution 22
8. Randy Savage: The Madness of Wrestling............................25
9. Triple H: The Game of Wrestling 28
10. Kurt Angle: Olympic Hero Turned Wrestling Icon 31
11. Eddie Guerrero: The Heart of Wrestling 34
12. Chris Jericho: The Ayatollah of Rock 'n' Rolla 37
13. Rey Mysterio: The Master of the 619 40
14. Daniel Bryan: The People's Underdog.................................43
15. Edge: The Rated-R Superstar..46
16. Jeff Hardy: The Enigmatic Daredevil...................................49
17. Ultimate Warrior: A Force of Nature in Wrestling............52
18. Ric Flair: The Nature Boy..55
19. CM Punk: The Voice of the Voiceless..................................58
20. Big Show: The Giant of Wrestling.......................................61
21. Mick Foley: The Hardcore Legend 64
22. Kane: The Big Red Machine 67
23. Booker T: From Struggles to Stardom.................................70
24. AJ Styles: The Phenomenal One...73
25. Randy Orton: The Apex Predator 76
26. Roman Reigns: The Tribal Chief..79
27. Seth Rollins: The Visionary 82
28. Dean Ambrose: The Lunatic Fringe.....................................85
29. Batista: The Animal Unleashed 88
30. Drew McIntyre: The Scottish Warrior 91

31. Finn Bálor: The Demon King..94
32. Kofi Kingston: The Ghanaian Sensation 97
33. Big E: The Powerhouse of Positivity 100
34. Xavier Woods: The Maestro of Positivity 103
35. Chris Benoit: The Wrestling Technician..................................... 106
36. Davey Boy Smith: The British Bulldog.. 109
37. Andre the Giant: The Eighth Wonder of the World 112
38. Goldberg: The Icon of Wrestling Power 115
39. AJ Lee: The Unstoppable Underdog 118
40. Trish Stratus: The Queen of Women's Wrestling 121
41. Lita: The Fearless Trailblazer... 124
42. Becky Lynch: Irish Lass Kicker 'The Man' 127
43. Charlotte Flair: The Queen of the Ring...................................... 130
44. Sasha Banks: The Boss of WWE 133
45. Bayley: The Hugger Who Transformed WWE 136
46. The Miz: From Reality Star to WWE Icon 139
47. Kevin Owens: The Relentless Prizefighter 142
48. Shinsuke Nakamura: The King of Strong Style 145
49. Braun Strowman: The Monster Among Men 148
50. Ricky Steamboat: The Dragon's Legacy 151
51. Dusty Rhodes: The American Dream 154
52. Bob Backlund: The Champion of Discipline............................. 157
53. Cody Rhodes: The Prince Who Became a King........................ 160
54. Roddy Piper: The Rowdy Rebel 163
55. Sting: The Icon of Wrestling... 166

Preface

Wrestling has always been more than just a sport. It is a theater of athleticism, storytelling, and drama where heroes rise, villains fall, and unforgettable moments are etched into history. From iconic rivalries to awe-inspiring feats of strength, the wrestling ring has been home to countless stories that transcend generations and cultures. This book, Legends of the Wrestling Ring, is a tribute to the men and women who have defined this world, shaping it into the cultural phenomenon we know today.

As fans of wrestling, we often marvel at the spectacle—the roaring crowds, the dramatic entrances, the finishing moves—but behind every wrestler is a story. These stories are filled with dreams, struggles, triumphs, and moments of reinvention. The idea of this book was born from a desire to capture these stories, to celebrate the lives of wrestling's greatest icons, and to present them in a way that connects with fans and newcomers alike.

The wrestlers featured in this book are not just athletes; they are storytellers, performers, and in many ways, larger-than-life figures. Each chapter dives into the life of a legend, chronicling their journey from humble beginnings to the grand stage of professional wrestling. We uncover their struggles and triumphs, the moments that defined their careers, and the legacies they left behind. Whether it's the enigmatic Sting, the rebellious Roddy Piper, or the visionary Paul Levesque, every story in this book is a testament to the enduring spirit of wrestling.

Why was this book written? Wrestling fans are a unique and passionate community. For many, these wrestlers are not just performers but role models and sources of inspiration. Their stories resonate because they reflect universal themes—perseverance in the face of adversity, the importance of staying true to oneself, and the courage to chase dreams no matter the odds. By documenting these tales, this book aims to preserve the rich history of professional wrestling and offer readers an intimate glimpse into the lives of their favorite superstars.

This book is not just a collection of biographies; it is a journey through time. From the golden era of wrestling to the modern-day spectacle, it showcases how the sport has evolved while staying true to its core. Each chapter highlights a different wrestler, offering insights into their personal lives, career-defining moments, and the challenges they overcame. We explore their rivalries, their most memorable matches, and the contributions they made to the industry.

For readers, this book offers something special. For die-hard wrestling fans, it is a nostalgic walk through memory lane, revisiting the legends who shaped their love for the sport. For newcomers, it is an introduction to the incredible world of wrestling and the figures who have made it iconic. Each chapter has been crafted to be engaging, informative, and accessible, making it an enjoyable read for anyone curious about the lives behind the personas.

But this book is not just about celebrating successes; it also delves into the struggles and sacrifices that come with a life in wrestling. Injuries, personal conflicts, and the physical and emotional toll of the sport are explored with honesty and sensitivity. These stories remind us that behind the face paint, championship belts, and flashy moves are real people with real challenges.

Legends of the Wrestling Ring is also a testament to the power of reinvention. Many wrestlers featured in this book faced setbacks—career-threatening injuries, personal struggles, or changes in the wrestling industry. Yet, they adapted, evolved, and came back stronger. Their journeys are not just about wrestling; they are about life, showing us that success often lies in perseverance and the willingness to keep moving forward, no matter the odds.

Readers will also find this book to be a source of inspiration. The lessons embedded in these stories go beyond the ring. Whether it's Dusty Rhodes' belief in the "American Dream," Cody Rhodes'

LEGENDS OF THE WRESTLING RING

commitment to carving his own path, or Roddy Piper's unapologetic individuality, each wrestler offers valuable insights that can inspire readers in their own lives.

Ultimately, this book was written for the fans. It is a celebration of the stories that have shaped professional wrestling, and an acknowledgment of the wrestlers who have given their all to entertain, inspire, and connect with audiences worldwide. It is also a reminder of the unity that wrestling creates—a sport that brings people together, transcending borders, languages, and generations.

In the pages of this book, readers will discover the lives of 55 legendary wrestlers, each with a unique story to tell. They will journey through the history of professional wrestling, exploring the eras, the rivalries, and the moments that have made it what it is today. They will learn about the sacrifices these athletes made to reach the pinnacle of their profession and the legacies they left behind.

So, whether you are a lifelong fan of wrestling or someone curious about the world of suplexes, powerbombs, and high-flying maneuvers, this book invites you to step into the ring and experience the magic of wrestling through the eyes of its greatest legends. It is a tribute to their dedication, their artistry, and the connection they have created with millions around the globe.

Legends of the Wrestling Ring is more than just a book—it is a celebration of a sport, an art form, and a community. May these stories inspire you, entertain you, and remind you of the power of dreams. Let the journey begin.

—**Author**

1. Steve Austin: The Journey of a Wrestling Legend

Steve Austin, known globally as "Stone Cold," was born on December 18, 1964, in Austin, Texas. From humble beginnings in Edna, a small Texas town, Steve grew up under the guidance of his mother and stepfather after his biological father left when he was just a year old. His mother, Beverly, and stepfather, Ken Williams, provided a stable environment where young Steve developed a strong work ethic and a love for sports. He excelled in football during high school and eventually earned a scholarship to the University of North Texas, where he played football and majored in physical education.

Despite a promising football career, Steve's passion for sports entertainment led him to wrestling. Inspired by legendary figures like Dusty Rhodes and Ric Flair, he decided to pursue professional wrestling, enrolling in Chris Adams' wrestling school in 1989. Austin's entry into the wrestling world wasn't smooth. His first fight took place in the small promotions of Texas, where he performed under the name "Steve Williams." Due to name conflicts with another wrestler, he adopted the moniker "Steve Austin," drawn from his stepfather's surname.

Steve's career gained traction in the United States Wrestling Association (USWA), where his technical skill and charisma began to shine. He joined World Championship Wrestling (WCW) in 1991, forming the tag team "The Hollywood Blonds" with Brian Pillman. Their partnership was short-lived but impactful, showcasing Steve's potential as a superstar. After a brief stint in Extreme Championship Wrestling (ECW), where his promo skills flourished, Austin joined the World Wrestling Federation (WWF) in 1995.

The turning point came in 1996 when he adopted the persona of "Stone Cold" Steve Austin. With a rebellious attitude, Austin broke away from traditional wrestling gimmicks, crafting a no-nonsense, beer-drinking, anti-authoritarian image that resonated with fans. His infamous catchphrase, "Austin 3:16 says I just whipped your ass," emerged after his victory against Jake Roberts in the King of the Ring tournament. This defining moment catapulted him into stardom, marking the beginning of the "Attitude Era" in professional wrestling.

Austin's career achievements are monumental. A six-time WWF Champion, two-time Intercontinental Champion, and four-time tag team champion, he was also the only wrestler to win three Royal Rumble matches (1997, 1998, 2001). His feuds with Vince McMahon, The Rock, and Triple H remain iconic, bringing unparalleled excitement to wrestling. Austin's in-ring style, characterized by brawling tactics and his signature move, the "Stone Cold Stunner," became synonymous with his dominance in the ring.

Despite his success, Austin faced challenges. A severe neck injury during a match with Owen Hart in 1997 nearly ended his career. Yet, his resilience saw him return stronger, albeit with a more conservative fighting style to protect his health. Another significant hurdle came in 2002 when he abruptly left WWE due to creative disagreements.

Although he returned later, it signaled the beginning of the end for his in-ring career.

Austin retired from active competition in 2003 following his WrestleMania XIX match against The Rock. Post-retirement, he continued to appear in WWE as an on-screen personality and special guest referee, maintaining his connection with fans. Outside wrestling, Austin pursued acting, starring in movies like "The Longest Yard" and "The Condemned," and hosted reality shows such as "Broken Skull Challenge." His podcast, "The Steve Austin Show," further solidified his status as a cultural icon.

Interestingly, Steve's on-screen persona of a beer-guzzling rebel contrasts with his off-screen discipline. Known for his humility and work ethic, he values authenticity and determination. He has often spoken about the importance of adapting to challenges and staying true to oneself, offering valuable insights for fans and aspiring wrestlers alike.

Steve Austin's journey is filled with intriguing anecdotes. For instance, his "Stone Cold" nickname was inspired by his then-wife's comment about drinking tea before it went stone cold. Lesser-known facts include his brief consideration of pursuing a music career and his fondness for hunting and ranching. These layers reveal a multifaceted personality beyond the wrestling ring.

Today, Steve Austin lives a quieter life on his ranch in Texas, enjoying the peace he earned after decades of hard work. Though retired, his legacy is, celebrated by fans worldwide. He remains a beloved figure in wrestling, an enduring symbol of resilience, rebellion, and the pursuit of excellence. As of now, Steve Austin is alive and well, continuing to inspire a new generation of wrestlers and fans.

2. Dwayne Johnson: A Legend Beyond the Ring

Dwayne "The Rock" Johnson was born on May 2, 1972, in Hayward, California. From his early years, it seemed destiny had something extraordinary in store for him. The son of wrestling legend Rocky Johnson and Ata Johnson, Dwayne grew up surrounded by the allure and challenges of professional wrestling. Despite his father's fame, the Johnson household faced its share of financial struggles, teaching Dwayne resilience from a young age.

As a child, Dwayne moved frequently due to his father's wrestling career, living in places as diverse as New Zealand and Pennsylvania. He struggled to find stability and often got into trouble. His parents, however, instilled a strong sense of discipline, and he soon channeled his energy into sports. He excelled in football during high school, earning a full scholarship to the University of Miami. There, he played defensive tackle and won a national championship in 1991, though injuries derailed his hopes of an NFL career.

When football no longer seemed viable, Dwayne turned to wrestling. His family's legacy played a significant role, but it wasn't an easy transition. Trained by his father and wrestling veterans, Dwayne debuted in the WWE (then WWF) in 1996 under the name "Rocky Maivia," a tribute to both his father and grandfather, Peter Maivia. His clean-cut, cheerful persona initially struggled to win over fans, leading to a barrage of boos. Frustrated but determined, Dwayne reinvented himself as "The Rock," a brash, charismatic, and sharp-tongued wrestler who quickly became a fan favorite.

The Rock's first notable match came at the Survivor Series in 1996, where he showcased his potential by being the sole survivor of his team. But his true breakthrough occurred in 1998 when he won his first WWF Championship against Mankind. From then on, his career skyrocketed, with memorable rivalries against Stone Cold Steve Austin, Triple H, and The Undertaker. His electrifying personality and iconic catchphrases like "If you smell what The Rock is cooking!" made him a household name.

Over his wrestling career, The Rock achieved unparalleled success. He held 10 world championships, multiple tag team titles, and was a two-time Intercontinental Champion. His matches, particularly those at WrestleMania, were legendary. With a total of over 1,700 matches, he won the majority, though his losses—such as those to Austin at WrestleMania XV and XVII—only added to his legacy by showcasing his ability to elevate his opponents.

The Rock's charisma wasn't confined to the ring. His transition to Hollywood began in 2001 with his role as the Scorpion King in "The Mummy Returns," leading to a standalone movie that launched his acting career. Balancing wrestling and movies, he eventually left the WWE in 2004 to focus full-time on acting. His performances in blockbusters like "Fast & Furious" and "Jumanji" solidified his status as a global superstar.

LEGENDS OF THE WRESTLING RING

Challenges were plenty for Dwayne. From dealing with injuries during his wrestling career to facing skepticism about his acting chops, he persevered with determination. Lesser-known stories, like his struggle with depression after his football dreams crumbled, reveal the depth of his resilience. Despite his fame, Dwayne remains grounded, often citing his humble beginnings and the lessons learned from failure.

Dwayne's life after wrestling is a testament to his multifaceted personality. Beyond acting, he is a successful entrepreneur, launching brands like Teremana Tequila and ZOA Energy. He is also deeply philanthropic, contributing to causes related to children's health and education. A dedicated father to his daughters, Dwayne often shares glimpses of his personal life, endearing him further to his fans.

Dwayne "The Rock" Johnson is very much alive and thriving. His journey from a struggling athlete to a wrestling icon, Hollywood superstar, and global inspiration is a story of grit, reinvention, and unwavering self-belief. Through every challenge and triumph, The Rock has proven that success isn't just about talent but also about perseverance, adaptability, and staying true to oneself.

3. Hulk Hogan: The Immortal Icon of Wrestling

Hulk Hogan, born Terry Eugene Bollea on August 11, 1953, in Augusta, Georgia, is one of the most recognizable and celebrated figures in professional wrestling history. Raised in Tampa, Florida, Terry grew up in a working-class family. His father, Pietro Bollea, was a construction foreman, and his mother, Ruth Bollea, was a homemaker and dance teacher. From an early age, Terry showed an interest in sports and music, excelling in baseball and later playing bass guitar in local bands.

Despite his athletic potential, injuries derailed his baseball aspirations, leading Terry to explore other avenues. He briefly attended the University of South Florida but dropped out to focus on his musical career. While performing with his band, he caught the attention of wrestling fans due to his massive 6'7" frame and muscular build. Local wrestlers persuaded him to try wrestling, and his journey into the world of sports entertainment began.

LEGENDS OF THE WRESTLING RING

Terry trained under wrestling legends Hiro Matsuda and Jack Brisco. His early days in the ring were marked by grueling training sessions designed to test his dedication. His professional wrestling debut came in 1977 as "The Super Destroyer," but it wasn't until he adopted the name "Hulk Hogan" that his career truly took off. The nickname came from his resemblance to the Marvel superhero Hulk and was cemented when he faced André the Giant in a local promotion.

Hogan's first major breakthrough occurred in 1979 when he joined the World Wrestling Federation (WWF). He gained national attention through his charismatic personality and incredible physique. His rivalry with André the Giant, which culminated in their legendary match at WrestleMania III, became a defining moment in wrestling history. Hogan body-slammed André in front of a record-breaking crowd, solidifying his status as a cultural icon.

Throughout the 1980s and early 1990s, Hogan was the face of the WWF. His signature moves, like the "Atomic Leg Drop," and his catchphrases, including "Whatcha gonna do, brother?" captivated audiences worldwide. Hogan's patriotism and larger-than-life persona resonated with fans, earning him the nickname "The Immortal." He held the WWF Championship five times during this period and headlined eight of the first nine WrestleManias.

Hulk Hogan's career wasn't without challenges. In the mid-1990s, his popularity waned as wrestling fans began favoring younger stars. Hogan made a bold move by joining World Championship Wrestling (WCW) in 1994, where he reinvented himself as a villain. His creation of the New World Order (nWo) faction, alongside Kevin Nash and Scott Hall, revitalized his career and helped WCW dominate the wrestling ratings.

Over his illustrious career, Hogan participated in over 2,000 matches, achieving more than 1,400 wins. While his losses were fewer, they were often in pivotal storylines designed to elevate his opponents. His rivalries with legends like Randy Savage, The Ultimate Warrior, and Ric Flair are still celebrated as some of the greatest feuds in wrestling.

Hogan's life outside the ring was just as eventful. He ventured into acting, starring in movies like "Rocky III" and "No Holds Barred." He also appeared in television shows and commercials, further cementing his status as a pop culture icon. However, his life was marked by controversies, including a high-profile legal battle with Gawker over a leaked tape. Despite these setbacks, Hogan emerged resilient, continuing to inspire fans with his perseverance.

One of the lesser-known stories about Hogan is his deep involvement in charity work. He has quietly supported children's hospitals and foundations for veterans, reflecting his belief in using fame for a greater purpose. Hogan often credits his parents for instilling values of hard work, humility, and generosity.

Hulk Hogan officially retired from wrestling in the early 2010s but continued to make appearances in WWE as a guest host and ambassador. His legacy lives on as the epitome of wrestling's golden era. Today, Hogan enjoys a quieter life in Clearwater, Florida, where he owns a beachside restaurant and spends time with his family.

As of now, Hulk Hogan is alive, his larger-than-life persona still shining in the hearts of fans worldwide. His story is a testament to the power of reinvention, resilience, and the pursuit of greatness. Hogan's journey from a struggling musician to a global icon is an inspiration to millions, proving that with determination and hard work, anyone can achieve the extraordinary.

4. John Cena: The Face That Runs the Place

John Cena, born on April 23, 1977, in West Newbury, Massachusetts, is a name synonymous with professional wrestling and perseverance. Raised in a large family as the second of five brothers, Cena's childhood was filled with competition and camaraderie. His father, John Cena Sr., worked as an announcer, while his mother, Carol Cena, managed the household. From a young age, Cena displayed an affinity for sports, idolizing action figures and superheroes, which laid the groundwork for his larger-than-life persona.

Cena attended Central Catholic High School before transferring to Cushing Academy, a private boarding school. He excelled in football, eventually earning a scholarship to Springfield College in Massachusetts. There, he played as a Division III All-American center on the football team and graduated with a degree in exercise physiology. His passion for fitness and dedication to personal development became the foundation of his journey into the world of professional wrestling.

After college, Cena moved to California to pursue a career in bodybuilding. While working as a limo driver to make ends meet, he was introduced to wrestling through Ultimate Pro Wrestling (UPW), a developmental promotion. Cena adopted the persona of "The Prototype," a half-human, half-machine character, showcasing his physical prowess and charisma. His dedication caught the attention of WWE scouts, and in 2001, Cena signed a developmental contract with Ohio Valley Wrestling (OVW).

Cena's WWE debut came on June 27, 2002, in a match against Kurt Angle. Although he lost, Cena's aggressive style and "ruthless aggression" caught the attention of fans and management alike. Over the next few years, he evolved from a generic rookie to the "Doctor of Thuganomics," a rapper who delivered insults in rhyme and connected with younger audiences. His transformation into a patriotic, never-give-up character solidified his place as a fan favorite.

John Cena's achievements in wrestling are unparalleled. He is a 16-time world champion, tying Ric Flair's record, and has won the Royal Rumble twice (2008, 2013). Cena has headlined numerous WrestleManias, including memorable bouts against The Rock, Triple H, and Edge. His rivalry with Randy Orton, spanning over a decade, is one of the most storied in WWE history. Known for his finishing move, the "Attitude Adjustment," and his resilience, Cena became the ultimate symbol of perseverance.

Over the course of his wrestling career, Cena has fought over 2,000 matches, with an impressive win-loss record that highlights his dominance. While he has faced defeats, including significant losses to stars like Brock Lesnar and CM Punk, these moments only added depth to his character. Cena's partnerships in tag teams, including his alliances with Shawn Michaels and Batista, also contributed to his legacy.

Cena's journey wasn't without challenges. Early in his career, he faced criticism for being too predictable in the ring. Yet, his unwavering dedication to entertaining fans helped him overcome these critiques. Injuries, including a torn pectoral muscle and neck surgery, threatened

LEGENDS OF THE WRESTLING RING

to derail his career, but Cena's remarkable recovery and return earned him admiration as a true fighter.

Beyond wrestling, Cena has carved a successful career in Hollywood, starring in blockbusters like "The Marine," "Trainwreck," and "Fast & Furious 9." His ability to transition seamlessly from wrestling to acting demonstrates his versatility and work ethic. Cena is also an author, having written books aimed at inspiring young readers.

One of Cena's most admirable qualities is his commitment to philanthropy. He holds the record for the most wishes granted through the Make-A-Wish Foundation, fulfilling over 650 wishes for children with critical illnesses. His dedication to spreading hope and positivity reflects his personal motto: "Never Give Up."

Lesser-known facts about Cena include his passion for collecting cars and boasting a garage filled with rare and custom-made vehicles. He is also fluent in Mandarin, a skill he developed to connect with WWE's Chinese fanbase. Cena's humility and willingness to embrace challenges set him apart, making him a role model for millions.

As of now, John Cena remains active in both wrestling and entertainment. While he has scaled back his WWE appearances, focusing more on acting, Cena occasionally returns to the ring to remind fans of his unparalleled legacy. Cena's story is far from over, and his contributions to wrestling and beyond ensure his name will echo for generations.

Cena continues to inspire people worldwide with his determination, kindness, and ability to adapt to new challenges. Whether in the ring, on the screen, or through his charitable work, Cena's life embodies the spirit of perseverance and the belief that hard work and a positive attitude can conquer any obstacle. His journey is a testament to the power of resilience, proving that true champions are not just defined by victories but by their impact on the world.

5. The Undertaker: The Phenom of Wrestling

The Undertaker, born Mark William Calaway on March 24, 1965, in Houston, Texas, is a name that commands respect and awe in the world of professional wrestling. Growing up in a close-knit family as the youngest of five brothers, Mark's childhood was filled with sports and camaraderie. His father, Frank Calaway, was a hardworking man, and his mother, Catherine, instilled values of humility and discipline in their children.

Mark attended Waltrip High School in Houston, where he excelled in basketball and football. His athletic abilities earned him a scholarship to Angelina College and later to Texas Wesleyan University, where he majored in sports management. While he initially pursued a career in basketball, his towering 6'10" frame and interest in combat sports led him to explore professional wrestling.

Mark's wrestling journey began in 1987, debuting under the ring name "Texas Red" in World Class Championship Wrestling (WCCW). His early matches, though unpolished, showcased his raw potential. After stints in various promotions, he joined World Championship Wrestling (WCW) as "Mean Mark Callous," but the character failed to gain traction. His fortunes changed in 1990 when he signed with the World Wrestling Federation (WWF, now WWE).

Debuting as "The Undertaker" at Survivor Series 1990, Mark adopted a dark, supernatural persona that would define his career. Clad in a black hat and trench coat, with a chilling entrance theme, The Undertaker became an instant sensation. His character was unique, blending intimidation with an aura of mystique, and his signature moves, including the "Tombstone Piledriver" and "Chokeslam," became legendary.

The Undertaker's achievements in WWE are unparalleled. He won seven world championships, the Royal Rumble in 2007, and held an astonishing 21-0 undefeated streak at WrestleMania, a record that cemented his legacy as "The Phenom." His rivalries with iconic wrestlers like Kane, Shawn Michaels, and Triple H produced some of the greatest matches in wrestling history.

Over his 30-year career, The Undertaker competed in more than 2,000 matches, with a remarkable win-loss record. While he faced losses, such as the end of his WrestleMania streak with Brock Lesnar in 2014, these moments only added to his character's depth. His partnerships, notably with Kane as "The Brothers of Destruction," showcased his versatility and loyalty as a performer.

The Undertaker's journey was not without challenges. He battled numerous injuries, including a broken orbital bone and hip replacements, yet continued to perform at the highest level. His ability to reinvent himself, from "The Deadman" to "The American Badass" and back, kept his character fresh and relevant for decades.

Mark's personal life also played a significant role in shaping his values. A devoted family man, he often credits his wife, Michelle McCool, for supporting him through the physical and emotional toll of his career.

Despite his on-screen persona, Mark is known for his humility and kindness, often mentoring younger wrestlers behind the scenes.

One of the lesser-known facts about The Undertaker is his love for motorcycles and mixed martial arts. He incorporated these interests into his "American Badass" gimmick in the early 2000s. Another interesting story is his dedication to kayfabe, maintaining his character's mystique even outside the ring for much of his career.

The Undertaker officially retired at Survivor Series 2020, exactly 30 years after his debut. His farewell was a poignant moment for fans worldwide, marking the end of an era. Post-retirement, Mark has focused on his family and business ventures, including a podcast and appearances at WWE events to share his wisdom and experiences.

As of now, Mark Calaway, better known as The Undertaker, is alive and well, enjoying a quieter life away from the ring. His legacy as a pioneer, mentor, and icon in wrestling remains unmatched. The Undertaker's story is a testament to the power of perseverance, reinvention, and the ability to leave an indelible mark on the hearts of millions. His journey continues to inspire fans and wrestlers alike, proving that legends truly never die.

6. Shawn Michaels: The Showstopper of Wrestling

Shawn Michaels, born Michael Shawn Hickenbottom on July 22, 1965, in Chandler, Arizona, is one of the most iconic figures in professional wrestling history. Raised in a military family, Shawn moved frequently during his childhood, eventually settling in San Antonio, Texas. His father, Richard, served in the Air Force, and his mother, Carol, managed the household. As the youngest of four siblings, Shawn learned early to stand out and entertain.

From a young age, Shawn was drawn to sports, particularly football. He excelled as a linebacker for Randolph High School, where his athleticism shone. Although he briefly attended Southwest Texas State University, he soon realized his passion lay outside academics. Inspired by his love for wrestling, Shawn decided to pursue a career in the ring, a decision that would shape his destiny.

Shawn began his wrestling journey at just 19 years old, training under the legendary Jose Lothario. His natural charisma and athleticism set him apart, and he made his professional debut in 1984 for the National

Wrestling Alliance (NWA). Wrestling as part of a tag team, he quickly gained recognition for his innovative moves and flair.

Shawn's big break came when he joined the American Wrestling Association (AWA) and later the World Wrestling Federation (WWF, now WWE) in 1988 as one-half of The Rockers, alongside Marty Jannetty. The duo's high-flying style captivated audiences, but their partnership ended dramatically in 1992 when Shawn turned on Marty, smashing him through a glass window during a segment on WWE's "The Barber Shop." This moment marked the birth of Shawn Michaels as "The Heartbreak Kid," a charismatic solo performer who would dominate the wrestling world.

Shawn's achievements in WWE are legendary. He is a four-time world champion, three-time Intercontinental Champion, and two-time Royal Rumble winner (1995, 1996). Known as "Mr. WrestleMania," Shawn delivered some of the greatest matches in wrestling history, including his bouts against The Undertaker, Bret Hart, and Razor Ramon. His ladder match against Razor Ramon at WrestleMania X set a new standard for athleticism and storytelling in wrestling.

Over his career, Shawn competed in over 1,700 matches, winning the majority. His losses, though rare, often came in iconic matches that elevated his opponents. Shawn's ability to tell a story in the ring, combined with his technical skill and charisma, earned him the nickname "The Showstopper."

Shawn's journey was not without challenges. In 1998, a back injury forced him to retire temporarily, and he struggled with personal demons, including addiction. However, his faith and family helped him turn his life around. Shawn's return to WWE in 2002 marked one of the greatest comebacks in wrestling history, culminating in unforgettable matches and rivalries.

Behind the scenes, Shawn was a controversial figure. His arrogance and outspoken nature earned him enemies, but his talent was undeniable.

LEGENDS OF THE WRESTLING RING

Despite past conflicts, Shawn matured over the years, earning respect as a mentor and leader in the locker room.

Lesser-known facts about Shawn include his passion for hunting and his role as a born-again Christian. He often credits his wife, Rebecca, and their two children for grounding him and giving him a purpose beyond wrestling. Shawn is also an avid supporter of charities, often using his platform to give back to the community.

Shawn officially retired in 2010 after his WrestleMania XXVI match against The Undertaker, a bout widely regarded as one of the best in wrestling history. Although he briefly returned for a match in 2018, Shawn has largely stayed out of the ring, focusing on coaching and mentoring younger wrestlers at WWE's Performance Center.

As of now, Shawn Michaels is alive and thriving, enjoying life as a family man and wrestling legend. His story is a testament to resilience, reinvention, and the pursuit of greatness. Shawn Michaels' legacy as The Heartbreak Kid, The Showstopper, and Mr. WrestleMania will forever echo in the annals of wrestling history, inspiring generations of fans and performers alike.

7. Bret Hart: The Excellence of Execution

Bret Hart, affectionately known as "The Hitman," was born on July 2, 1957, in Calgary, Alberta, Canada. His story is deeply intertwined with the history of professional wrestling. Bret grew up as the eighth of twelve children in the legendary Hart family, headed by his father, Stu Hart, a renowned wrestler and trainer, and his mother, Helen Hart. The Hart household was not just a family home—it was a wrestling institution, with a basement famously known as "The Dungeon," where Stu trained countless wrestling hopefuls.

Bret's childhood revolved around wrestling, but he initially harbored dreams of becoming a filmmaker. He attended Ernest Manning High School, excelling in amateur wrestling, and later enrolled at Mount Royal College to study filmmaking. However, wrestling soon pulled him into its orbit. As a young man, Bret started refereeing matches for his father's promotion, Stampede Wrestling. Before long, he stepped into the ring himself, and his natural talent was undeniable.

Bret's professional wrestling debut came in 1976 in Stampede Wrestling. Initially reluctant, he quickly discovered his knack for technical wrestling. His first matches showcased his methodical

LEGENDS OF THE WRESTLING RING

approach and ability to tell compelling stories in the ring. Bret's skill caught the attention of World Wrestling Federation (WWF) scouts, and in 1984, he signed with the company.

In WWF, Bret formed the tag team "The Hart Foundation" with his brother-in-law, Jim "The Anvil" Neidhart. Managed by Jimmy Hart, the duo won multiple tag team championships and became fan favorites for their contrasting styles—Bret's precision balanced by Neidhart's raw power. Bret's singles career began to take shape in the late 1980s, and he quickly rose to prominence, earning the moniker "The Excellence of Execution" for his flawless technique.

Bret's achievements are nothing short of remarkable. A five-time WWF Champion, two-time Intercontinental Champion, and two-time King of the Ring winner, he solidified his legacy with memorable matches against legends like Shawn Michaels, Stone Cold Steve Austin, and Mr. Perfect. His WrestleMania XIII bout against Austin, often considered one of the greatest wrestling matches of all time, showcased his ability to adapt and elevate his opponents.

Over his career, Bret wrestled in over 2,000 matches, achieving more than 1,500 victories. While he experienced defeats, including controversial losses like the infamous "Montreal Screwjob" in 1997, these moments only added depth to his story. The Screwjob, where Vince McMahon orchestrated Bret's loss to Shawn Michaels without his knowledge, remains a pivotal and controversial moment in wrestling history, symbolizing the complexities of the business.

Despite his success, Bret faced immense challenges. The death of his brother, Owen Hart, during a wrestling stunt in 1999, profoundly affected him. Additionally, a career-ending concussion in 1999 forced Bret to step away from wrestling. A stroke in 2002 further tested his resilience, but Bret made an incredible recovery, eventually returning to WWE in 2010 for a Hall of Fame induction and a final storyline.

Lesser-known facts about Bret reveal his depth as a person. A talented artist, he has illustrated his own memoirs and written extensively about his life. Bret is also a passionate advocate for wrestlers' rights, emphasizing safety and fair treatment in the industry. His humility and honesty have endeared him to fans worldwide.

Bret officially retired from wrestling in the early 2000s but remained active in various capacities, including mentoring younger wrestlers and appearing at WWE events. Today, he lives in Calgary with his family, focusing on his legacy and philanthropic efforts.

As of now, Bret Hart is alive and well, celebrated as one of the greatest technical wrestlers in history. His story is a testament to the power of dedication, perseverance, and staying true to one's principles. Bret's journey, filled with triumphs and trials, serves as an inspiration to millions, proving that excellence is achieved through passion and hard work. The Hitman's legacy will forever be etched in the annals of professional wrestling.

8. Randy Savage: The Madness of Wrestling

Randy Mario Poffo, better known as Randy "Macho Man" Savage, was born on November 15, 1952, in Columbus, Ohio. Wrestling greatness seemed to run in the family. His father, Angelo Poffo, was a professional wrestler, and his younger brother, Lanny Poffo, also made a name in the wrestling world. Growing up, Randy displayed an unmatched enthusiasm for sports, particularly baseball, and wrestling. His mother, Judy, supported the boys' ambitions while ensuring they remained grounded.

Randy attended Downers Grove North High School in Illinois, where he excelled in sports, particularly baseball. After graduation, he pursued a baseball career, playing as an outfielder in the minor leagues for teams affiliated with the St. Louis Cardinals and Cincinnati Reds. However, injuries hindered his path to Major League Baseball. During his recovery, he began exploring professional wrestling, following in his father's footsteps.

Randy's wrestling career began in the 1970s, wrestling under the name "The Spider." His high-flying moves and unmatched energy set him apart. It wasn't long before he adopted the name Randy Savage, suggested by a promoter who believed it suited his intense style. The "Macho Man" persona followed soon after, and with it came the flamboyant robes, sunglasses, and cowboy hats that would become his trademarks.

Savage's first major success came in the International Championship Wrestling (ICW), a promotion run by his father. However, his big break arrived in the early 1980s when he joined the World Wrestling Federation (WWF). His debut match against Rick McGraw in 1985 showcased his explosive athleticism and undeniable charisma. Paired with his real-life wife and manager, Miss Elizabeth, Savage became an instant sensation.

Randy's achievements in wrestling are legendary. He was a two-time WWF Champion, a four-time WCW World Heavyweight Champion, and an Intercontinental Champion. His matches, including the iconic WrestleMania III bout against Ricky "The Dragon" Steamboat, are considered some of the best in wrestling history. Known for his finishing move, the "Flying Elbow Drop," Savage combined technical skill with showmanship, making him one of the most versatile wrestlers of his era.

Over his career, Savage fought in over 1,700 matches, with an impressive win-loss record. His rivalries with Hulk Hogan, Ultimate Warrior, and Ric Flair were filled with drama and intensity, captivating audiences worldwide. He also formed memorable alliances, including the Mega Powers with Hulk Hogan, though their partnership famously ended in a fiery feud.

Behind the scenes, Savage faced many challenges. His obsessive dedication to perfection often led to conflicts with other wrestlers. He was known to rehearse his matches meticulously, striving for excellence in every performance. His relationship with Miss Elizabeth, both on and off-screen, was central to his storylines but eventually strained under the pressures of fame and personal struggles.

LEGENDS OF THE WRESTLING RING

One of the lesser-known stories about Savage is his passion for music. In 2003, he released a rap album, "Be a Man," showcasing his creative flair outside the ring. Another interesting fact is his appearance in the 2002 film "Spider-Man," where he played the wrestler Bonesaw McGraw, introducing him to a new generation of fans.

Savage retired from full-time wrestling in 2000 but made sporadic appearances in the ring and continued to inspire fans with his larger-than-life persona. He shifted his focus to acting, endorsements, and enjoying a quieter life with his second wife, Lynn Payne, in Florida. Tragically, on May 20, 2011, Randy Savage passed away after suffering a heart attack while driving. His car crashed into a tree in Seminole, Florida, but his wife, who was with him, survived the accident. His sudden death shocked the wrestling world, and tributes poured in from fans and wrestlers alike, honoring the legacy of the Macho Man.

Randy "Macho Man" Savage remains one of the most beloved and influential figures in wrestling history. His unmatched charisma, dedication to his craft, and unforgettable performances have left an indelible mark. Even in his absence, the spirit of the Madness lives on, reminding fans to embrace passion, individuality, and the pursuit of excellence. Ooh yeah!

9. Triple H: The Game of Wrestling

Triple H, born Paul Michael Levesque on July 27, 1969, in Nashua, New Hampshire, is a name synonymous with power, strategy, and dominance in the world of professional wrestling. Raised in a middle-class family, Paul grew up with a deep passion for bodybuilding and athletics. His father, Paul Levesque Sr., worked as a businessman, while his mother, Patricia, was a homemaker who supported her son's ambitions.

From a young age, Paul was captivated by professional wrestling, idolizing stars like Ric Flair and Harley Race. He attended Nashua South High School, where he excelled in sports. By the age of 14, he began bodybuilding, earning accolades in local competitions. His dedication to fitness paved the way for a career in the spotlight, but it was his larger-than-life persona that made him a star.

After graduating, Paul attended college briefly while continuing his bodybuilding career. His efforts caught the attention of Walter "Killer" Kowalski, a wrestling legend who ran a school for aspiring wrestlers. Under Kowalski's tutelage, Paul learned the art of wrestling and debuted in 1992 under the ring name Terra Ryzing in independent promotions. His technical skill and charisma were evident, and soon he was signed by World Championship Wrestling (WCW).

In WCW, Paul adopted the name Jean-Paul Lévesque, portraying a snobbish French aristocrat. While the gimmick showed his ability to embody a character, WCW failed to utilize his potential. In 1995, Paul left WCW to join the World Wrestling Federation (WWF, now WWE), where he rebranded himself as Hunter Hearst Helmsley, a Connecticut blueblood with a pompous attitude.

Triple H's first significant feud was against Henry O. Godwinn, culminating in a memorable match in 1995. His early career in WWE was a mix of mid-card feuds and tag team bouts, but his fortunes changed when he aligned with Shawn Michaels to form D-Generation X (DX) in 1997. The faction, known for its rebellious and edgy antics, became a cornerstone of WWE's "Attitude Era." Triple H's leadership and charisma propelled him into the main event scene.

As a solo performer, Triple H's career flourished. Known as "The Game" and "The Cerebral Assassin," he dominated the WWE landscape, winning 14 world championships and becoming a two-time Royal Rumble winner (2002, 2016). His rivalries with The Rock, Stone Cold Steve Austin, The Undertaker, and Kurt Angle are legendary. Matches like the Hell in a Cell bout against Mick Foley and his WrestleMania clashes with The Undertaker showcased his ability to deliver unforgettable performances.

Over his career, Triple H competed in over 2,000 matches, with an impressive win-loss record. His alliances, including Evolution with Ric Flair, Randy Orton, and Batista, and The Authority with Stephanie McMahon, reinforced his status as a mastermind in and out of the ring. His signature moves, like the Pedigree, became iconic symbols of his dominance.

Behind the scenes, Triple H faced significant challenges. His 2001 quadriceps injury during a tag match nearly ended his career, but his grueling rehabilitation and triumphant return earned him widespread respect. As WWE's Executive Vice President of Talent, Live Events, and Creative, he played a pivotal role in launching NXT, WWE's developmental brand, nurturing the next generation of superstars.

Triple H's personal life is equally fascinating. He married Stephanie McMahon, daughter of WWE Chairman Vince McMahon, in 2003. The couple's partnership extended beyond their personal lives, shaping WWE's creative direction and business strategy. Triple H's dedication to his family and the wrestling industry reflects his belief in hard work, loyalty, and innovation.

Lesser-known facts about Triple H include his love for heavy metal music, which inspired his entrance themes, and his admiration for bodybuilding legend Arnold Schwarzenegger. Despite his on-screen persona as a calculating villain, Triple H is known for his generosity and mentorship behind the scenes.

Triple H's career milestones are numerous, but his impact on wrestling goes beyond championships. His ability to reinvent himself, adapt to changing eras, and elevate others has cemented his legacy as one of the greatest wrestlers of all time. His speeches and interviews often emphasize the importance of perseverance, strategy, and passion, values he embodies to this day.

In 2022, Triple H officially retired from in-ring competition due to health concerns, following a cardiac event that required surgery. While he no longer competes, his influence on WWE remains profound as he continues to shape its future through his executive role.

As of now, Paul Levesque, better known as Triple H, is alive and thriving. His journey from a young boy dreaming of wrestling glory to a global icon is a testament to hard work, vision, and resilience. Triple H's story inspires fans worldwide, proving that true greatness lies in the ability to evolve, lead, and leave a lasting impact. The King of Kings continues to reign in the hearts of wrestling fans everywhere.

10. Kurt Angle: Olympic Hero Turned Wrestling Icon

Kurt Angle, born on December 9, 1968, in Mt. Lebanon Township, Pennsylvania, is a name that shines brightly in both amateur and professional wrestling. From an early age, Kurt displayed a natural talent for sports and a relentless determination to succeed. His parents, Jackie and David Angle, raised him alongside his four older brothers and a sister in a supportive yet hardworking environment. Tragically, Kurt's father passed away in a construction accident when Kurt was only 16, leaving a void that fueled his drive to honor his family.

Kurt attended Mt. Lebanon High School, where he excelled in football and wrestling. His passion for wrestling grew stronger as he competed in national tournaments, earning recognition for his discipline and skill. He later attended Clarion University of Pennsylvania, where he became a two-time NCAA Division I Wrestling Champion. Kurt's college years were a testament to his unyielding work ethic and desire to be the best.

In 1996, Kurt achieved the ultimate accolade in amateur wrestling: an Olympic gold medal at the Atlanta Games. What made this feat extraordinary was that he won the medal with a broken neck, a testament to his grit and determination. His victory became a symbol of resilience and paved the way for his transition into professional wrestling.

Kurt's professional wrestling career began in 1998 when he signed with World Wrestling Federation (WWF, now WWE). Initially skeptical about the entertainment aspect of wrestling, Kurt quickly adapted, debuting in 1999 with his patriotic "American Hero" persona. His first match, a victory against Shawn Stasiak, showcased his ability to blend technical wrestling with charisma, earning him the admiration of fans.

Over the years, Kurt Angle amassed an impressive list of achievements. He became a six-time world champion in WWE, winning the WWE Championship four times and the World Heavyweight Championship twice. He also captured the Intercontinental and European Championships and won the 2000 King of the Ring tournament. Kurt's matches against icons like Stone Cold Steve Austin, Brock Lesnar, and Shawn Michaels are still considered classics, with his WrestleMania XIX bout against Lesnar being a standout.

Kurt's wrestling career wasn't limited to WWE. In 2006, he joined Total Nonstop Action Wrestling (TNA), where he continued to dominate, winning multiple world championships and solidifying his legacy as one of the best wrestlers of all time. His ability to adapt to different styles and opponents showcased his versatility and cemented his reputation as a technical master.

Despite his successes, Kurt faced numerous challenges. The toll of wrestling and his Olympic journey led to multiple injuries, including a broken neck on several occasions. Additionally, Kurt struggled with addiction to painkillers, a battle he bravely overcame with rehabilitation and support from his family.

LEGENDS OF THE WRESTLING RING

Lesser-known facts about Kurt reveal his multifaceted personality. He once considered pursuing an NFL career and even had offers but chose to stay true to his wrestling roots. Kurt is also an accomplished actor, appearing in films like "Warrior" and TV shows such as "Psych." His humility and sense of humor have endeared him to fans, making him relatable despite his larger-than-life accomplishments.

Kurt retired from in-ring competition in 2019, with his final match taking place at WrestleMania 35 against Baron Corbin. While the match wasn't the grand farewell fans had hoped for, Kurt's legacy as an Olympic hero and wrestling legend remains untarnished. Post-retirement, Kurt has focused on motivational speaking, acting, and spending time with his wife, Giovanna, and their five children.

As of now, Kurt Angle is alive and thriving, continuing to inspire people with his story of perseverance and triumph. His journey from a young boy in Pennsylvania to an Olympic gold medalist and wrestling icon serves as a reminder that with determination, resilience, and a never-give-up attitude, anything is possible. Kurt Angle's legacy as the "Wrestling Machine" and a true American hero will forever be celebrated in the world of sports and beyond.

11. Eddie Guerrero: The Heart of Wrestling

Eddie Guerrero, born Eduardo Gory Guerrero Llanes on October 9, 1967, in El Paso, Texas, was a wrestler whose charisma, skill, and resilience left an indelible mark on the world of professional wrestling. Eddie was born into the legendary Guerrero wrestling family, headed by his father, Gory Guerrero, a renowned luchador and trainer. Growing up, Eddie was surrounded by wrestling, with his brothers and uncles also competing in the ring. His mother, Herlinda, ensured the family remained close-knit despite the demands of the wrestling world. Eddie's early life was steeped in the traditions of lucha libre. From a young age, he dreamed of following in his father's footsteps. He attended Jefferson High School in El Paso, where he excelled in athletics, and later went on to study at the University of New Mexico. However, the call of the wrestling ring was too strong, and Eddie began training under his father's watchful eye.

Eddie's professional wrestling career began in Mexico, where he honed his craft in promotions like CMLL and AAA. His high-flying moves, combined with technical precision, made him a standout performer. Eddie's first major success came in 1994 when he joined Extreme

LEGENDS OF THE WRESTLING RING

Championship Wrestling (ECW), where he captivated audiences with his matches against Dean Malenko. His talent soon caught the attention of World Championship Wrestling (WCW), where he became a fan favorite despite being underutilized.

In 2000, Eddie made the move to the World Wrestling Federation (WWF, now WWE), where his career truly took off. He joined forces with Chris Benoit, Dean Malenko, and Perry Saturn as The Radicalz, a group of former WCW stars. Eddie's charm and comedic timing quickly set him apart, and his "Latino Heat" persona became one of the most beloved characters in WWE history.

Eddie's achievements in WWE were numerous. He won the Intercontinental Championship, the United States Championship, and multiple tag team titles. However, his crowning moment came in 2004 when he defeated Brock Lesnar to win the WWE Championship at No Way Out. The victory was a testament to Eddie's journey from underdog to world champion and remains one of the most emotional moments in wrestling history.

Over his career, Eddie competed in over 2,000 matches, with a remarkable win-loss record. His rivalries with stars like Rey Mysterio, Kurt Angle, and JBL showcased his versatility, while his partnerships with Chavo Guerrero and Batista highlighted his ability to connect with others in and out of the ring.

Despite his success, Eddie's journey was fraught with challenges. He battled addiction to painkillers and alcohol, struggles that nearly derailed his career. In 2001, he was released from WWE due to these issues, but his determination to rebuild his life brought him back stronger than ever. Eddie's return to WWE in 2002 marked the beginning of a career resurgence, as he became a role model for redemption and perseverance.

Lesser-known facts about Eddie include his love for music and drawing, hobbies he often used to unwind. He was deeply devoted to his family, especially his wife, Vickie, and their three daughters.

Eddie's faith played a significant role in his life, guiding him through his struggles and shaping his outlook.

Tragically, Eddie Guerrero passed away on November 13, 2005, in Minneapolis, Minnesota, due to heart failure caused by underlying health issues. His death shocked the wrestling world, and tributes poured in from fans and colleagues alike. WWE dedicated episodes of Raw and SmackDown to his memory, celebrating his legacy.

Eddie Guerrero's story is one of resilience, passion, and love for wrestling. His ability to entertain, inspire, and connect with fans made him a legend. Eddie's legacy lives on in the hearts of wrestling fans, a reminder that true greatness comes not just from victories but from the courage to overcome life's challenges. Viva La Raza!

12. Chris Jericho: The Ayatollah of Rock 'n' Rolla

Chris Jericho, born Christopher Keith Irvine on November 9, 1970, in Manhasset, New York, is one of the most versatile and influential figures in professional wrestling. Raised in Winnipeg, Manitoba, Canada, Chris grew up in a household that valued sports and creativity. His father, Ted Irvine, was a professional hockey player in the NHL, and his mother, Loretta, supported the family's passions while instilling a love for the arts in Chris.

Chris was drawn to professional wrestling at a young age, inspired by legendary performers like Shawn Michaels and Ricky Steamboat. He attended Red River College in Winnipeg, earning a degree in Creative Communications, which later shaped his ability to connect with audiences. While many of his peers pursued conventional careers, Chris's heart was set on entertaining the world.

His journey into wrestling began in 1990, when he trained at the Hart Brothers School of Wrestling, under the guidance of Stu Hart's family. Alongside fellow trainee Lance Storm, Chris debuted in the Canadian independent circuit as part of a tag team, showing early signs of his unique charisma and athleticism. His first official match took place in Ponoka, Alberta, and although he didn't win, his performance hinted at the greatness to come.

Chris's early career was a whirlwind of travel and opportunity. He competed in promotions like CMLL in Mexico, WAR in Japan, and ECW in the United States. However, his big break came in 1996 when he joined World Championship Wrestling (WCW). As "Lionheart" Chris Jericho, he quickly gained a reputation for his technical skill and ability to cut entertaining promos.

In 1999, Chris signed with the World Wrestling Federation (WWF, now WWE), making one of the most memorable debuts in wrestling history by interrupting The Rock. This moment marked the arrival of "Y2J," a brash and charismatic persona that propelled him to stardom. Over the years, Chris became a nine-time Intercontinental Champion, a six-time world champion, and the first-ever Undisputed Champion, unifying the WWF and WCW titles in 2001 by defeating The Rock and Stone Cold Steve Austin on the same night.

Jericho's versatility extended beyond wrestling. He formed the rock band Fozzy, showcasing his talents as a musician and frontman. Balancing wrestling and music, Chris built a career that transcended the ring, earning admiration for his ability to reinvent himself. His catchphrases like "You just made the list!" and "Drink it in, man" became iconic, cementing his connection with fans.

Over his career, Chris has competed in over 2,000 matches, with a stellar win-loss record. His rivalries with The Rock, Triple H, and Kevin Owens are some of the most celebrated in wrestling history. Equally impressive are his alliances, including his stints with The Inner Circle in AEW and Jericho Appreciation Society, which showcased his leadership and mentoring abilities.

Jericho's career has had its challenges. From navigating the politics of WCW to dealing with the physical toll of decades in the ring, Chris faced every obstacle with determination. His ability to adapt, whether it was by changing his persona or exploring new ventures, reflects his resilience and creativity.

Lesser-known facts about Chris reveal his intellectual curiosity and entrepreneurial spirit. He is a best-selling author, having written multiple autobiographies that offer insights into his journey. He also hosts a successful podcast, "Talk Is Jericho," where he interviews guests from various fields, showcasing his passion for storytelling and connection.

Despite his enduring success, Jericho remains grounded, often crediting his family for keeping him focused. Married to Jessica Lockhart since 2000, he is a devoted father to their three children and a role model for balancing fame with family life.

Chris Jericho's impact on wrestling extends beyond championships. He is a pioneer of reinvention, proving that staying relevant requires courage and innovation. Whether as Y2J, The Painmaker, or The Wizard, Jericho continues to captivate audiences, blending humor, intensity, and unpredictability.

As of now, Chris Jericho remains active in All Elite Wrestling (AEW), mentoring young talent while delivering top-tier performances. His story is a testament to passion, hard work, and the belief that success comes from constantly challenging oneself. Chris Jericho is more than a wrestler; he is a cultural icon whose legacy will inspire generations to come.

13. Rey Mysterio: The Master of the 619

Rey Mysterio, born Óscar Gutiérrez on December 11, 1974, in Chula Vista, California, is a name that has redefined the world of professional wrestling. Known for his high-flying moves, colorful masks, and unrelenting determination, Rey has captivated fans for decades, earning a legacy as one of the most beloved wrestlers of all time.

Growing up in a Mexican-American family, Rey was introduced to the traditions of lucha libre by his uncle, Rey Misterio Sr., a renowned luchador. From a young age, Rey dreamed of following in his uncle's footsteps. Despite his small stature, he was undeterred, believing that skill and heart could overcome any physical limitations. His parents, Roberto and Maria, supported his ambitions, instilling values of hard work and perseverance.

Rey began training under his uncle at the age of 14, learning the art of lucha libre in Tijuana, Mexico. He made his professional debut at just 15 years old in 1989, wrestling under the name "Colibrí." Although he didn't win his first match, Rey's agility and innovative style made an impression. His uncle eventually gave him the name Rey Mysterio Jr., a nod to the family's wrestling legacy.

LEGENDS OF THE WRESTLING RING

Rey's career gained momentum in Mexico's AAA promotion, where his matches against Psicosis and Juventud Guerrera showcased his incredible athleticism and storytelling ability. In 1995, Rey joined Extreme Championship Wrestling (ECW) in the United States, introducing American audiences to his unique blend of lucha libre and high-risk maneuvers. His success in ECW led to an opportunity with World Championship Wrestling (WCW) in 1996.

During his time in WCW, Rey became a fan favorite, known for his breathtaking moves like the "Hurricanrana" and "Springboard Moonsault." Despite facing larger opponents, Rey's underdog spirit resonated with fans. He won the Cruiserweight Championship multiple times and had memorable rivalries with Eddie Guerrero, Chris Jericho, and Dean Malenko.

In 2002, Rey signed with World Wrestling Entertainment (WWE), where he adopted the nickname "The Master of the 619," named after his finishing move and San Diego's area code. Rey's WWE debut was electrifying, and he quickly became a cornerstone of the company's SmackDown brand. His matches against Kurt Angle, Edge, and The Undertaker solidified his reputation as one of the best in-ring performers of his generation.

Rey's crowning achievement came in 2006 when he won the Royal Rumble, entering at number two and lasting over an hour to secure victory. This win set the stage for his triumph at WrestleMania 22, where he defeated Randy Orton and Kurt Angle to become World Heavyweight Champion. The victory was a tribute to his late friend Eddie Guerrero, whose memory inspired Rey to reach new heights.

Over his career, Rey has competed in thousands of matches, winning numerous championships, including the WWE Championship, Intercontinental Championship, and Tag Team Championships. His partnerships with Eddie Guerrero, Batista, and Dominik Mysterio have been highlights of his journey, showcasing his ability to connect with fans and fellow wrestlers alike.

Rey's career was not without challenges. He suffered multiple knee injuries that required surgeries, forcing him to adapt his style. Additionally, he faced the pressure of balancing his family life with the demands of a global wrestling career. Despite these obstacles, Rey's resilience and love for wrestling kept him going.

Lesser-known facts about Rey include his passion for tattoo art, with many of his tattoos symbolizing his family and heritage. Rey is also deeply spiritual, often dedicating his victories to his faith. His humility and gratitude have made him a role model for fans around the world.

Rey has yet to officially retire, continuing to compete in WWE alongside his son, Dominik. Their tag team matches symbolize the passing of the torch and the continuation of the Mysterio legacy. Rey's journey is a testament to the power of determination, proving that size is no barrier to greatness.

As of now, Rey Mysterio remains active and beloved in the wrestling world. His story inspires fans to dream big, work hard, and never give up. Rey's legacy as a pioneer of lucha libre and a global icon ensures his place in wrestling history for generations to come. The Master of the 619 will forever be remembered as a champion of heart and spirit.

14. Daniel Bryan: The People's Underdog

Daniel Bryan, born Bryan Lloyd Danielson on May 22, 1981, in Aberdeen, Washington, is a wrestler who has defined resilience and passion in the world of professional wrestling. Growing up in a small logging town, Bryan was the son of a therapist mother, Darlene, and a logger father, Donald. His parents separated when he was young, but Bryan found solace in his love for sports and the outdoors, often helping his father with tough physical labor.

Bryan attended Aberdeen-Weatherwax High School, where he played football and participated in track and field. Despite his athletic abilities, he was drawn to professional wrestling after being inspired by stars like Shawn Michaels. Determined to pursue his dream, Bryan saved up and enrolled in the Texas Wrestling Academy, where he trained under Shawn Michaels and Rudy Boy Gonzalez. It was here that Bryan developed the technical skills and work ethic that would make him a legend.

Bryan's first professional match came in 1999 at the age of 18. Wrestling in local promotions and using the name "American Dragon," he quickly gained a reputation for his technical precision and ability to adapt to any opponent. His journey took him across the globe, competing in Japan, the United Kingdom, and the United States for promotions like Ring of Honor (ROH), where he became the inaugural ROH Pure Wrestling Champion and later the ROH World Champion.

Bryan's WWE career began in 2010 as part of the first season of NXT, a reality-based competition show. Despite being eliminated early, his talent and connection with fans were undeniable. After debuting on the main roster, Bryan captured the United States Championship, but it was his underdog journey that truly resonated with fans.

The turning point in Bryan's career came in 2013 during his feud with The Authority, WWE's on-screen management team. The storyline portrayed Bryan as an overlooked underdog, echoing his real-life struggles to prove himself in an industry dominated by larger-than-life athletes. Fans rallied behind him with the "Yes!" The movement was a collective chant that became a global phenomenon.

Bryan's crowning achievement occurred at WrestleMania 30 in 2014. After defeating Triple H in the opening match, Bryan went on to win a triple-threat main event against Batista and Randy Orton, capturing the WWE World Heavyweight Championship. The moment, marked by Bryan's emotional celebration with fans and family, solidified him as one of WWE's greatest underdog champions.

Throughout his career, Bryan has won multiple championships, including five world titles, the Intercontinental Championship, the United States Championship, and multiple tag team titles. He has wrestled over 1,700 matches, earning the respect of fans and peers for his ability to deliver show-stopping performances against opponents of all sizes and styles.

However, Bryan's journey has not been without challenges. In 2016, he was forced to retire due to concussion-related injuries, a devastating moment for him and his fans. During his retirement, Bryan served as General Manager of SmackDown and focused on his personal life,

LEGENDS OF THE WRESTLING RING

including becoming a father to two children with his wife, Brie Bella, a WWE Hall of Famer.

Remarkably, Bryan returned to in-ring competition in 2018 after extensive rehabilitation and medical clearance. His comeback marked one of the most emotional moments in wrestling history, as he proved that determination and perseverance could overcome even the toughest obstacles.

Bryan's lesser-known passions include environmentalism and veganism, causes he actively supports. He is known for his humble lifestyle, often advocating for sustainability and mindfulness. Bryan's connection with fans stems from his authenticity and commitment to staying true to his values.

As of now, Daniel Bryan, known as Bryan Danielson in All Elite Wrestling (AEW), continues to compete at a high level, inspiring fans worldwide with his technical brilliance and unwavering passion for wrestling. His story is a testament to the power of hard work, belief, and the ability to turn setbacks into comebacks.

Daniel Bryan's legacy as the ultimate underdog proves that size and odds don't matter when you have heart and determination. The "Yes!" The movement will forever symbolize his journey, inspiring generations to fight for their dreams, no matter the challenges.

15. Edge: The Rated-R Superstar

Edge, born Adam Joseph Copeland on October 30, 1973, in Orangeville, Ontario, Canada, is a wrestler whose journey is a testament to resilience and passion. Raised by his single mother, Judy Copeland, Adam grew up in modest circumstances, learning the value of hard work and perseverance. His father left before he was born, and his mother worked multiple jobs to support them, becoming Adam's biggest inspiration.

From an early age, Adam was drawn to wrestling, idolizing stars like Hulk Hogan and Bret Hart. He attended Orangeville District Secondary School, where he excelled in academics and sports. Despite his passion for wrestling, Adam knew the importance of education and promised his mother he would prioritize his studies while pursuing his dream.

Adam's entry into wrestling began when he won an essay contest at the age of 17, earning free training at Sully's Gym in Toronto. Under the mentorship of Ron Hutchison and Sweet Daddy Siki, he honed his craft, debuting in 1992 on the Canadian independent circuit.

LEGENDS OF THE WRESTLING RING

Wrestling under various aliases, Adam's charisma and athleticism quickly caught the attention of promoters.

His big break came in 1997 when he signed with the World Wrestling Federation (WWF, now WWE). Adopting the ring name "Edge," he debuted on television in 1998 with a mysterious, brooding character. His first major storyline involved his partnership with Christian, his real-life best friend. Together, they formed one of the most iconic tag teams in wrestling history.

Edge and Christian's comedic timing and high-flying moves made them fan favorites. Their TLC (Tables, Ladders, and Chairs) matches against the Hardy Boyz and Dudley Boyz are legendary, setting new standards for innovation and risk-taking in the ring. The duo won the Tag Team Championship seven times, solidifying their place in WWE history.

As a singles competitor, Edge's career skyrocketed. Known as "The Rated-R Superstar," he embraced a controversial and edgy persona, becoming one of WWE's top heels. His rivalry with John Cena, his Money in the Bank cash-in moments, and his multiple World Heavyweight Championship wins cemented his legacy. Edge was a master of storytelling, capable of evoking both cheers and boos with ease.

Throughout his career, Edge amassed an impressive list of achievements. He became an 11-time world champion, a five-time Intercontinental Champion, and a 14-time Tag Team Champion. He also won the Royal Rumble twice (2010 and 2021), showcasing his ability to overcome the odds.

However, Edge's journey was not without challenges. In 2011, he was forced to retire due to cervical spinal stenosis, a condition that put him at risk of paralysis if he continued wrestling. His retirement speech on Raw was emotional, marking the end of an era. Fans and peers celebrated his contributions, and he was inducted into the WWE Hall of Fame in 2012.

Despite stepping away from the ring, Edge remained active in the entertainment world, appearing in movies and TV shows like Haven and Vikings. He also focused on his family life with his wife, WWE Hall of Famer Beth Phoenix, and their two daughters.

In a remarkable twist of fate, Edge returned to wrestling in 2020 after nearly a decade of retirement. Cleared to compete following extensive rehabilitation, he made a shocking comeback at the Royal Rumble. His return was a testament to his resilience and love for wrestling, and he continued to deliver standout performances against stars like Randy Orton, Roman Reigns, and Seth Rollins.

Lesser-known facts about Edge include his love for music, particularly heavy metal, and his passion for comic books. His entrance theme, "Metalingus" by Alter Bridge, became one of the most iconic in wrestling history. Edge is also known for his humility, often crediting his success to his mother's sacrifices and his fans' unwavering support.

As of now, Edge remains an active competitor, proving that age and setbacks are no barriers to greatness. His story is a testament to the power of passion, hard work, and the belief that it's never too late to chase your dreams. Edge's legacy as the ultimate opportunist and a master storyteller ensures his place among wrestling's greatest legends.

16. Jeff Hardy: The Enigmatic Daredevil

Jeff Hardy, born Jeffrey Nero Hardy on August 31, 1977, in Cameron, North Carolina, is a name synonymous with daredevilry and innovation in professional wrestling. Growing up in a small town, Jeff was raised by his father, Gilbert Hardy, after the passing of his mother, Ruby Moore Hardy, when Jeff was just nine years old. The loss of his mother deeply influenced Jeff and his older brother, Matt, strengthening their bond and fueling their creative energy.

As a child, Jeff was a multi-talented athlete, excelling in motocross, baseball, and football. His fascination with art and music also set him apart. He attended Union Pines High School, where he developed a love for performing and expressing himself creatively. Despite his varied interests, wrestling remained his ultimate passion, inspired by stars like Shawn Michaels and Sting.

Jeff's journey into professional wrestling began in the early 1990s, alongside his brother Matt. Together, they created their own wrestling promotion, the Trampoline Wrestling Federation (TWF), which served as a training ground for their innovative high-flying style. They eventually joined the independent circuit, wrestling for promotions like the Organization of Modern Extreme Grappling Arts (OMEGA), which they co-founded.

In 1998, Jeff and Matt signed with the World Wrestling Federation (WWF, now WWE). Known as The Hardy Boyz, the duo became trailblazers in the tag team division. Their high-risk moves, such as Jeff's Swanton Bomb and Matt's Twist of Fate, thrilled audiences. Their battles in TLC (Tables, Ladders, and Chairs) matches against The Dudley Boyz and Edge & Christian are legendary, redefining what tag team wrestling could be.

Jeff's solo career flourished in the 2000s. Known as "The Charismatic Enigma," he captured the WWE Championship, World Heavyweight Championship, and Intercontinental Championship. His feuds with The Undertaker, Triple H, and CM Punk showcased his ability to connect with fans through both his athleticism and his underdog persona.

Throughout his career, Jeff has competed in over 2,000 matches, achieving numerous victories and earning a reputation as one of the most creative and fearless performers in wrestling history. However, his journey was not without challenges. Jeff faced struggles with addiction and injuries, leading to multiple hiatuses from WWE. Despite these setbacks, he always managed to make remarkable comebacks, demonstrating his resilience and love for the sport.

One of the most significant turning points in Jeff's career came in 2009 when he won his first WWE Championship. The moment was a culmination of years of hard work and perseverance, cementing his place among wrestling's elite. Fans rallied behind Jeff, admiring his authenticity and ability to overcome personal and professional obstacles.

Outside the ring, Jeff is a man of many talents. He is an accomplished musician, leading the band PeroxWhy?Gen, and a skilled artist known for his abstract paintings and sculptures. These creative outlets reflect his enigmatic personality, which has always been a key part of his appeal.

Jeff's lesser-known facts include his love for animals and his role as a father to two daughters. He is deeply committed to his family and often credits them for grounding him. Despite his larger-than-life persona, Jeff remains humble, valuing his connection with fans above all else.

In 2022, Jeff joined All Elite Wrestling (AEW), reuniting with Matt to rekindle their iconic partnership. While he continues to perform, Jeff has hinted at a future beyond the ring, focusing on his creative passions and spending more time with his family.

Jeff Hardy's legacy is one of innovation, resilience, and inspiration. His story proves that even in the face of adversity, passion and determination can lead to greatness. The Charismatic Enigma will forever be remembered as a pioneer in wrestling, captivating fans with his fearless spirit and unyielding drive to entertain.

17. Ultimate Warrior: A Force of Nature in Wrestling

The Ultimate Warrior, born James Brian Hellwig on June 16, 1959, in Crawfordsville, Indiana, was one of the most intense and unforgettable characters in the world of professional wrestling. Raised in a working-class family, Jim was the eldest of five children. His parents divorced when he was young, and his mother, Mary, worked tirelessly to provide for the family. Despite the challenges, Jim developed a strong sense of independence and a desire to succeed.

As a teenager, Jim was drawn to athletics, particularly weightlifting and bodybuilding. He attended Fountain Central High School, where his passion for fitness set him apart. After graduating, he briefly attended Indiana State University, studying chiropractic medicine, but his heart was elsewhere. His love for physical competition and personal growth led him to pursue bodybuilding full-time.

Jim's dedication paid off when he won the AAU Mr. Georgia bodybuilding competition in 1984. During this time, he was introduced to wrestling by a group of bodybuilders who were transitioning into the sport. Intrigued by the larger-than-life personas and physical demands of wrestling, Jim decided to give it a try.

Jim began his wrestling career in 1985, training under Red Bastien and working in small promotions under the name "Blade Runner Rock." Teaming with Steve Borden, who would later become Sting, the duo gained attention as The Blade Runners. Their partnership didn't last long, but Jim's potential was evident. He soon rebranded himself as "The Dingo Warrior" in World Class Championship Wrestling (WCCW), where his energy and intensity began to captivate audiences.

In 1987, Jim signed with the World Wrestling Federation (WWF) and adopted the name "The Ultimate Warrior." With his face painted in bold colors, tassels adorning his arms, and a frenetic entrance that saw him sprint to the ring, Warrior became an instant sensation. His unrelenting energy and wild persona were unlike anything fans had seen before.

Warrior's rise to stardom was meteoric. His matches were characterized by their sheer intensity, and his feuds with legends like Hulk Hogan, "Macho Man" Randy Savage, and Rick Rude became the stuff of wrestling lore. At WrestleMania VI in 1990, Warrior achieved his greatest triumph, defeating Hogan to become the WWF Champion in a title-versus-title match. The victory solidified him as a top star and a hero to millions of fans.

Throughout his career, Warrior amassed numerous accolades, including two WWF Intercontinental Championships and a reign as WWF Champion. He wrestled over 1,000 matches, with an impressive win-loss record that showcased his dominance in the ring. Despite his success, Warrior's career was not without controversy. His larger-than-life persona sometimes clashed with the business side of wrestling, leading to several high-profile disputes with management.

One of Warrior's greatest challenges was maintaining his personal and professional life amid the pressures of fame. He left WWF multiple times during his career, each departure marked by rumors and speculation. Despite these setbacks, Warrior always found a way to return, fueled by his unwavering belief in his character and message.

Lesser-known facts about Warrior include his passion for motivational speaking and writing. After retiring from wrestling in the late 1990s, he legally changed his name to Warrior and dedicated himself to inspiring others through his philosophy of self-reliance and personal empowerment. His colorful personality extended beyond the ring, making him a polarizing yet fascinating figure.

In 2014, The Ultimate Warrior was inducted into the WWE Hall of Fame, a moment that brought closure to his tumultuous relationship with the industry. Just days later, on April 8, 2014, Warrior passed away suddenly from a heart attack in Scottsdale, Arizona. His death shocked the wrestling world, occurring so soon after his emotional return to WWE.

Warrior's legacy is one of passion, individuality, and perseverance. He remains an enduring symbol of the power of self-belief and the courage to stand out. The Ultimate Warrior's story reminds fans that greatness is achieved not just through victories but through the impact one leaves behind. His spirit, energy, and message will forever be remembered in the annals of wrestling history.

18. Ric Flair: The Nature Boy

Ric Flair, born Richard Morgan Fliehr on February 25, 1949, in Memphis, Tennessee, is one of the most iconic and influential figures in the history of professional wrestling. Adopted as an infant by Dr. Richard and Kathleen Fliehr, Ric was raised in Edina, Minnesota. His adoptive parents provided a comfortable life, with his father working as a physician and his mother managing their home.

As a child, Ric was an energetic and mischievous boy with a knack for entertaining. He attended Wayland Academy, a boarding school in Wisconsin, where he developed an interest in athletics, excelling in football, wrestling, and track. After high school, Ric enrolled at the University of Minnesota but soon dropped out to pursue a career in professional wrestling, a decision that would define his life.

Ric's wrestling journey began in 1972 when he trained under Verne Gagne, a legendary promoter and wrestler. Gagne's rigorous training camp was grueling, but Ric's natural charisma and athletic ability shone through. He debuted later that year in the American Wrestling Association (AWA), showing promise with his flamboyant persona and in-ring skill.

In 1974, Ric's career nearly ended before it began. A devastating plane crash left him with a broken back and doctors doubting he'd ever wrestle again. Refusing to give up, Ric endured intense physical therapy and made an astonishing comeback in 1975. This resilience became a hallmark of his career.

Ric joined Jim Crockett Promotions, which later became World Championship Wrestling (WCW), and transformed into "The Nature Boy." Inspired by Buddy Rogers, Ric embraced the glamorous persona with his trademark sequined robes, "Wooo!" catchphrase, and extravagant lifestyle. His charisma and technical wrestling ability made him a superstar.

Ric's achievements in wrestling are unparalleled. He is recognized as a 16-time world champion, having held the NWA, WCW, and WWF World Heavyweight Championships. His matches against legends like Dusty Rhodes, Ricky Steamboat, and Sting are considered masterpieces of storytelling and athleticism. The trilogy of matches with Steamboat in 1989 remains a benchmark for excellence in wrestling.

Throughout his career, Ric wrestled thousands of matches, earning victories against the best in the business. His losses, often as part of dramatic storylines, only added to his legend. As the leader of the Four Horsemen, one of wrestling's most iconic factions, Ric redefined what it meant to be a villain, balancing arrogance with undeniable talent.

Ric's career wasn't without challenges. His lavish lifestyle, which mirrored his on-screen persona, led to financial troubles and personal setbacks. Multiple marriages and a strained relationship with his children added to his struggles. Despite these obstacles, Ric remained a beloved figure, known for his humility and ability to connect with fans. One of the most significant turning points in Ric's career came in 1992 when he joined the World Wrestling Federation (WWF). He immediately made an impact by winning the Royal Rumble and becoming WWF Champion. His versatility allowed him to succeed in any promotion, cementing his status as a global star.

Lesser-known facts about Ric include his love for music and his appearances in pop culture, from rap songs to TV shows. His influence extended beyond wrestling, inspiring athletes, entertainers, and fans with his flamboyant persona and dedication to his craft.

Ric officially retired from in-ring competition in 2008 after an emotional match against Shawn Michaels at WrestleMania 24. The moment, marked by Shawn's iconic "I'm sorry, I love you" line, was a fitting end to Ric's legendary career. However, like many wrestlers, Ric couldn't stay away from the ring and made sporadic appearances in promotions like TNA.

In 2012, Ric's contributions to wrestling were immortalized when he became a two-time WWE Hall of Fame inductee, both as an individual and as a member of the Four Horsemen. His legacy as one of the greatest wrestlers of all time remains undisputed.

As of now, Ric Flair is alive and continues to entertain fans with his appearances and stories. His journey from a struggling athlete to the Nature Boy is a testament to resilience, charisma, and the power of reinvention. Ric Flair's legacy will forever shine as one of wrestling's brightest stars. Wooo!

19. CM Punk: The Voice of the Voiceless

CM Punk, born Phillip Jack Brooks on October 26, 1978, in Chicago, Illinois, is a name that resonates with rebellion, authenticity, and passion in professional wrestling. Growing up in Lockport, a suburb of Chicago, Punk was raised in a working-class family. His father struggled with alcoholism, a challenge that shaped Punk's values of self-discipline and independence. He became a staunch advocate of the straight-edge lifestyle, abstaining from alcohol, drugs, and smoking—a principle that would define his persona inside and outside the ring.

Punk's early love for wrestling was sparked by watching stars like Roddy Piper and Bret Hart. Attending Lockport Township High School, he was drawn to alternative subcultures like punk rock, which influenced his attitude and style. After graduation, Punk began training at the Steel Domain Wrestling School in Chicago, under Ace Steel and Danny Dominion. Wrestling came naturally to him, but his unique personality and relentless drive set him apart from others.

Punk's professional wrestling debut came in 1999 on the independent circuit, where he quickly gained a reputation for his technical prowess and sharp wit. Wrestling for IWA Mid-South and Ring of Honor

(ROH), Punk honed his craft in grueling matches against top talent like Samoa Joe. His 60-minute time-limit draws with Joe are legendary, showcasing his endurance and storytelling ability. ROH became Punk's proving ground, where his straight-edge lifestyle became a core part of his character, sparking rivalries and captivating audiences.

In 2005, CM Punk signed with WWE, starting in their developmental territory, Ohio Valley Wrestling (OVW). His charisma and in-ring ability quickly elevated him, and he debuted on WWE's main roster in 2006 as part of the ECW brand. Punk's straight-edge persona clashed with WWE's larger-than-life characters, but his authenticity and connection with fans made him a standout.

Punk's WWE career was marked by groundbreaking achievements. He won the ECW Championship, and multiple World Heavyweight Championships, and became a two-time Money in the Bank winner—the only wrestler to win it in consecutive years. His 434-day reign as WWE Champion from 2011 to 2013 is one of the longest in modern history. Matches against John Cena, Daniel Bryan, and The Undertaker showcased Punk's ability to deliver on the biggest stages.

The turning point in Punk's career came on June 27, 2011, with the infamous "Pipe Bomb" promo. Sitting cross-legged on the stage, Punk aired his grievances with WWE management and corporate politics, blurring the line between reality and fiction. This moment catapulted him into superstardom, earning him the moniker "The Voice of the Voiceless." Fans rallied behind Punk, viewing him as a symbol of rebellion against the status quo.

Despite his success, Punk faced significant challenges. He often clashed with WWE management over creative decisions, feeling undervalued despite his contributions. The physical toll of wrestling and frustration with the company's direction led Punk to leave WWE in 2014. His departure sent shockwaves through the wrestling world, and fans were left wondering if they'd ever see him in a wrestling ring again.

Outside of wrestling, Punk explored other ventures. He pursued a career in mixed martial arts, signing with the UFC in 2014. Though his MMA career was short-lived, Punk's willingness to step outside his comfort zone showcased his fearless nature. He also delved into writing comic books and made appearances in movies and TV shows, proving his versatility as an entertainer.

One of Punk's lesser-known passions is his love for animals, particularly his rescue dog, Larry. Punk is also a vocal advocate for mental health awareness, often encouraging fans to embrace authenticity and seek help when needed. His dedication to his values, even in the face of adversity, has made him a role model for many.

In 2021, after a seven-year hiatus, CM Punk made a triumphant return to wrestling with All Elite Wrestling (AEW). His debut on AEW Rampage in his hometown of Chicago remains one of the most emotional and celebrated moments in wrestling history. Punk's return reignited his connection with fans, proving that his legacy is as strong as ever.

As of now, CM Punk remains active in AEW, continuing to inspire fans with his uncompromising spirit and passion for wrestling. His journey from a rebellious kid in Chicago to a global wrestling icon is a testament to the power of authenticity, hard work, and staying true to one's beliefs.

CM Punk's story is not just about championships and accolades—it's about fighting for what you believe in and never settling for less. His legacy as "The Best in the World" is a reminder that greatness comes from the courage to challenge the norm and speak out for those who cannot. CM Punk is more than a wrestler; he is a voice, a fighter, and a symbol of defiance that will echo for generations.

20. Big Show: The Giant of Wrestling

Big Show, born Paul Donald Wight II on February 8, 1972, in Aiken, South Carolina, is one of the most recognizable figures in professional wrestling. Known for his immense size and surprising agility, Paul has carved a legendary career in the ring, captivating audiences worldwide. Paul's early life was marked by a medical condition called acromegaly, which caused excessive growth. By the time he was 12, he stood 6 feet 2 inches tall and weighed over 220 pounds. Despite the challenges associated with his condition, Paul excelled in sports like basketball and football during his high school years. His parents, Paul Sr. and Patricia Wight supported his aspirations, encouraging him to channel his size and strength into athletics. Paul underwent surgery in his late teens to remove a tumor on his pituitary gland, effectively halting the progression of his condition.

After high school, Paul attended Wichita State University on a basketball scholarship. His towering frame and athletic prowess made him a standout player, but his true calling lay outside the basketball court. A chance meeting with wrestling legend Hulk Hogan in 1994 led to an introduction to World Championship Wrestling (WCW), where Paul's journey as a professional wrestler began.

In 1995, Paul debuted in WCW under the ring name "The Giant," billed as the son of André the Giant. His debut match at Halloween Havoc was nothing short of extraordinary—he defeated Hulk Hogan to win the WCW World Heavyweight Championship. The victory established Paul as a dominant force in wrestling, and his career took off from there.

In 1999, Paul signed with the World Wrestling Federation (WWF, now WWE) and adopted the name "Big Show." His debut at St. Valentine's Day Massacre: In Your House marked the beginning of an illustrious WWE career. Big Show's combination of size, strength, and surprising agility made him a unique performer. He could lift opponents with ease, execute high-impact moves, and even perform top-rope maneuvers.

Big Show's achievements in WWE are remarkable. He is a seven-time world champion, having won the WWE, WCW, and ECW Championships. He also captured multiple tag team and mid-card titles, becoming one of the most decorated wrestlers in history. His rivalries with stars like The Undertaker, Brock Lesnar, and John Cena showcased his ability to adapt to different opponents and storylines.

Despite his success, Big Show faced numerous challenges. His size often made him the subject of unfair expectations, and injuries took a toll on his body. Balancing his larger-than-life persona with his personal life was another hurdle, but Paul's resilience and professionalism helped him overcome these obstacles.

One of the turning points in Big Show's career came in the mid-2000s when he transitioned to a more comedic role, showcasing his versatility. Matches like his infamous Sumo match against Akebono at WrestleMania 21 and his feud with Floyd Mayweather Jr. highlighted his willingness to entertain fans in unconventional ways.

LEGENDS OF THE WRESTLING RING

Big Show's lesser-known talents include acting, with appearances in films like The Waterboy and Knucklehead, and TV shows such as The Big Show Show on Netflix. He is also known for his charitable work, often visiting children's hospitals and supporting various causes.

In 2021, Big Show joined All Elite Wrestling (AEW), adopting his real name, Paul Wight, and continuing to contribute to the industry as both a wrestler and commentator. His transition to AEW marked a new chapter in his career, proving his enduring love for wrestling.

Big Show's legacy is one of resilience, adaptability, and dedication. His journey from a young boy grappling with a rare condition to a global wrestling icon is a testament to his strength and determination. Paul Wight's story inspires fans to embrace their uniqueness and pursue their dreams, no matter the challenges. The Giant's legacy will forever loom large in the annals of wrestling history.

21. Mick Foley: The Hardcore Legend

Mick Foley, born Michael Francis Foley on June 7, 1965, in Bloomington, Indiana, is one of the most unique and beloved figures in professional wrestling. Known for his incredible toughness, creativity, and humor, Foley carved out a legacy that transcended the sport, becoming an icon of resilience and storytelling.

Mick grew up in East Setauket, New York, in a modest home with his parents, Beverly and Jack Foley. His father was an athletic director, and his mother was a homemaker. Mick was an imaginative child who loved sports and comic books, often dreaming of becoming a superhero. He attended Ward Melville High School, where he played lacrosse and wrestled. His passion for wrestling ignited during his teenage years, inspired by Jimmy Snuka's high-flying antics.

Foley attended SUNY Cortland, where he studied communications. It was during college that Mick began seriously considering a wrestling career. He famously created a homemade wrestling video, in which he performed daring stunts like jumping off his roof onto mattresses. This tape, now legendary among fans, showcased Foley's dedication to entertaining others, even at great personal risk.

LEGENDS OF THE WRESTLING RING

Mick's professional wrestling career began in 1983 when he trained under Dominic DeNucci in Pennsylvania. Wrestling as Cactus Jack, Foley made a name for himself on the independent circuit, competing in promotions like World Class Championship Wrestling (WCCW) and World Championship Wrestling (WCW). His hardcore style, which included brutal matches involving barbed wire, thumbtacks, and flaming tables, earned him a cult following.

Foley's first major break came in WCW, where his character Cactus Jack thrived. He feuded with stars like Sting and Vader, delivering matches that pushed the boundaries of physical endurance. His 1993 match against Vader, where he lost part of his ear due to an accident, is a testament to his willingness to sacrifice for the sake of storytelling.

In 1996, Foley joined the World Wrestling Federation (WWF, now WWE), debuting as the deranged Mankind. This character, complete with a leather mask and haunting demeanor, showcased Foley's versatility as a performer. Mankind's dark, yet oddly endearing personality connected with fans, and his feuds with The Undertaker and Stone Cold Steve Austin became legendary.

One of the most iconic moments in Foley's career occurred at King of the Ring 1998, during his Hell in a Cell match against The Undertaker. Foley was thrown off the top of the cell, crashing through the announcer's table—a moment that left fans and wrestlers alike in shock. Despite injuries, Foley continued the match, cementing his reputation as the "Hardcore Legend."

Foley's achievements in WWE include three WWE Championships, eight tag team championships, and a Hardcore Championship reign that solidified his legacy in that division. His characters, including Mankind, Cactus Jack, and Dude Love, showcased his ability to reinvent himself while staying true to his core identity.

Beyond the ring, Foley's humor and intelligence shone through. He became a best-selling author, penning autobiographies like Have a Nice Day! And children's books that endeared him to fans of all ages. His work as a motivational speaker and advocate for charities further demonstrated his depth as a person.

Lesser-known facts about Foley include his love for Christmas, which led him to become a real-life Santa Claus during the holidays. He is also a devoted family man, often sharing stories about his wife, Colette, and their four children. Foley's humility and kindness have made him a fan favorite both in and out of the ring.

Foley officially retired from full-time wrestling in 2000 but made sporadic appearances in WWE and other promotions. His post-wrestling career has included acting, writing, and advocating for social causes. Despite stepping away from the ring, Foley's impact on wrestling remains profound.

Mick Foley's story is one of resilience, creativity, and heart. His willingness to endure pain for the sake of entertainment and his ability to connect with fans on a personal level makes him one of the most beloved figures in wrestling history. Foley's legacy as the Hardcore Legend is a reminder that greatness comes not from physical perfection but from the courage to be yourself and give your all to what you love. Have a nice day!

22. Kane: The Big Red Machine

Kane, born Glenn Thomas Jacobs on April 26, 1967, in Torrejon de Ardoz, Spain, is one of the most iconic and enduring figures in professional wrestling. Born on a U.S. Air Force base to American parents, Glenn grew up in a disciplined yet supportive environment. His family eventually settled in Missouri, where Glenn spent his formative years. A bright and athletic child, Glenn excelled academically and athletically, playing basketball and football in high school.

Glenn attended Northeast Missouri State University (now Truman State University), where he earned a degree in English literature. During his college years, he also played basketball, using his towering 6'8" frame to his advantage. However, his passion for storytelling and performing led him to pursue a career in professional wrestling.

Glenn's wrestling journey began in 1992 when he trained under Ray Candy and wrestled in the independent circuit under various ring names, including "Doomsday" and "Unabomb." He eventually caught the attention of World Championship Wrestling (WCW) and Smoky Mountain Wrestling (SMW), where he partnered with Al Snow to win the SMW Tag Team Championship. Despite these early successes, it wasn't until Glenn joined the World Wrestling Federation (WWF, now WWE) that his career truly took off.

In WWE, Glenn initially wrestled under several forgettable gimmicks, including "Dr. Isaac Yankem, DDS" and "Fake Diesel." However, his big break came in 1997 when he was introduced as Kane, the deranged and vengeful brother of The Undertaker. Kane's debut at the Bad Blood: In Your House pay-per-view, where he ripped the door off a Hell in a Cell to confront The Undertaker, remains one of the most dramatic moments in wrestling history.

Kane's storyline with The Undertaker became the backbone of his career. Their love-hate relationship, marked by epic feuds and alliances, captivated fans for decades. Matches like their WrestleMania 14 bout and the first-ever Inferno Match showcased Kane's ability to deliver unforgettable performances. The two also formed one of the most dominant tag teams in WWE history, The Brothers of Destruction, winning multiple championships together.

Kane's achievements in WWE are staggering. He is a three-time world champion, a 12-time tag team champion, and a two-time Intercontinental Champion. He also holds the record for the most Royal Rumble match eliminations in history, a testament to his longevity and dominance. Kane's versatility allowed him to excel in both singles and tag team competitions, and his ability to adapt kept him relevant across multiple eras of wrestling.

One of Kane's most significant moments came in 2010 when he won the Money in the Bank ladder match and cashed in the contract the same night to defeat Rey Mysterio for the World Heavyweight Championship. This victory marked the pinnacle of his career, cementing his legacy as a main-event performer.

Behind the scenes, Glenn Jacobs is known for his intelligence, humility, and professionalism. He is deeply respected by his peers and fans alike for his dedication to the wrestling industry. Lesser-known facts about

LEGENDS OF THE WRESTLING RING

Glenn include his passion for politics and community service. In 2018, Glenn was elected as the mayor of Knox County, Tennessee, showcasing his ability to connect with people beyond the wrestling world.

Kane's journey was not without challenges. His monstrous persona required intense physicality, leading to injuries and a grueling schedule. Despite these hardships, Kane remained a constant presence in WWE, reinventing his character to stay relevant. His comedic side was also evident in storylines like his partnership with Daniel Bryan as "Team Hell No," which showcased his versatility and humor.

Kane officially transitioned to a part-time wrestling role in the late 2010s, focusing more on his responsibilities as mayor. His sporadic appearances in WWE continue to delight fans, proving that the Big Red Machine still has plenty of fuel left.

As of now, Kane remains an active public figure, balancing his political career with occasional wrestling appearances. His story is a testament to hard work, adaptability, and the power of reinvention. Kane's legacy as one of the most fearsome and enduring characters in wrestling history will forever burn brightly in the hearts of fans.

23. Booker T: From Struggles to Stardom

Booker T, born Booker Tio Huffman Jr. on March 1, 1965, in Houston, Texas, is one of the most dynamic and inspiring figures in professional wrestling. His journey from a challenging childhood to becoming a global wrestling icon is a story of resilience, determination, and raw talent.

Booker was the youngest of eight siblings, raised by his mother, Lois after his father passed away when he was just ten months old. Tragedy struck again when his mother died of complications from a stroke when Booker was 13. Left orphaned, Booker was taken in by his older sister. Despite the difficulties, he found solace in sports and a deep bond with his brother, Stevie Ray, who would later play a pivotal role in his wrestling career.

In high school, Booker excelled in football and basketball. After graduating, he faced financial struggles and made decisions that landed him in trouble with the law. He spent 19 months in prison for armed robbery, a turning point that motivated him to change his life. Determined to build a better future, Booker found work as a security guard and later as a warehouse worker.

LEGENDS OF THE WRESTLING RING

Booker's introduction to wrestling came through his brother, Stevie Ray. Encouraged by Stevie, Booker trained at Ivan Putski's wrestling school in Houston. His natural athleticism and charisma were evident from the start. He debuted in 1989, wrestling for small promotions under the ring name "G.I. Bro." Though the gimmick was short-lived, it marked the beginning of a remarkable career.

In 1993, Booker and Stevie Ray joined World Championship Wrestling (WCW) as the tag team Harlem Heat. Managed by Sister Sherri, the duo became one of the most dominant tag teams in wrestling history, winning a record ten WCW World Tag Team Championships. Their success showcased Booker's versatility, blending power, speed, and showmanship.

Booker's singles career took off in the late 1990s. He captured the WCW World Television Championship six times, a testament to his consistency and work ethic. His rise to the top culminated in 2000 when he won the WCW World Heavyweight Championship, solidifying his status as a main-event star. Booker's ability to connect with fans, combined with his electrifying moves like the Scissors Kick and Spinaroonie, made him a fan favorite.

When WCW was acquired by WWE in 2001, Booker transitioned to the new company. His WWE debut was memorable, attacking Stone Cold Steve Austin at the King of the Ring pay-per-view. Though the WCW invasion storyline was controversial, Booker's talent shone through. He won multiple championships, including the World Heavyweight Championship, United States Championship, and Intercontinental Championship.

One of the defining moments of Booker's career came in 2006 when he adopted the "King Booker" persona. After winning the King of the Ring tournament, Booker transformed into a regal character, complete with a faux British accent and a queen by his side (his wife, Sharmell). The gimmick was a hit, earning him the WWE World Heavyweight

Championship and a place in fans' hearts as one of the most entertaining characters of the era.

Booker's achievements are remarkable. He is a six-time world champion, a 15-time tag team champion, and a two-time Hall of Fame inductee (individually and as part of Harlem Heat). His rivalries with The Rock, Triple H, and Chris Benoit produced some of the best matches of his career.

Despite his success, Booker faced challenges. Early in his career, he struggled with self-doubt and navigating the politics of the wrestling industry. However, his resilience and positive attitude helped him overcome these obstacles. He credits his family, particularly his wife Sharmell, for keeping him grounded.

Outside the ring, Booker is a man of many talents. He founded Reality of Wrestling, a wrestling school and promotion in Texas, dedicated to mentoring the next generation of wrestlers. His autobiography, From Prison to Promise: Life Before the Squared Circle, chronicles his journey from hardship to triumph. Booker is also a skilled commentator, adding insight and humor to WWE broadcasts.

Lesser-known facts about Booker include his passion for gaming and his love for martial arts. He holds a black belt in Brazilian jiu-jitsu and often incorporates his skills into his matches. Booker's philanthropic efforts, including community outreach programs and charity events, highlight his commitment to giving back.

As of now, Booker remains active as a mentor, commentator, and occasional in-ring performer. His story is a testament to the power of redemption, proving that with determination and a strong support system, anyone can rise above adversity.

Booker T's legacy as a wrestler and role model is secure. His journey from a troubled youth to a celebrated icon inspires fans around the world, reminding them to always aim high and never give up. Can you dig that, sucka?

24. AJ Styles: The Phenomenal One

AJ Styles, born Allen Neal Jones on June 2, 1977, in Camp Lejeune, North Carolina, is one of the most gifted and dynamic wrestlers in the history of professional wrestling. Growing up in a military family, Allen was the youngest of four boys. His father served in the Marine Corps, and his family often struggled financially. Despite these hardships, his parents instilled in him a strong work ethic and resilience.

Raised in Gainesville, Georgia, Allen's childhood was far from easy. His father battled alcoholism, and the family faced financial instability. Despite these challenges, Allen found solace in sports, particularly wrestling and football. A natural athlete, he attended Johnson High School, where he excelled in athletics. He later attended Anderson University in South Carolina on a partial wrestling scholarship but left early to focus on his passion for professional wrestling.

Allen's journey into wrestling began with humble origins. In 1998, he trained under Rick Michaels at a wrestling school in Georgia. Allen quickly showcased his raw talent and determination, debuting in 1999 under the ring name "AJ Styles." His first match, in a small independent promotion, ended in defeat, but it was the start of a journey that would take him to global stardom.

AJ's big break came in 2002 when he joined Total Nonstop Action Wrestling (TNA, now Impact Wrestling). He became the face of the promotion, winning the X Division Championship and elevating the division with his innovative, high-flying style. AJ's matches against Samoa Joe, Christopher Daniels, and Kurt Angle are considered classics, with his rivalry against Daniels and Joe in 2005 becoming a benchmark for modern wrestling.

Styles' achievements in TNA were unparalleled. He became a five-time TNA World Heavyweight Champion and a six-time X Division Champion, solidifying his status as the cornerstone of the promotion. His agility, precision, and ability to connect with fans earned him the nickname "The Phenomenal One."

In 2014, AJ made a significant career move, joining New Japan Pro-Wrestling (NJPW). As a member of the Bullet Club, AJ became a global sensation, capturing the IWGP Heavyweight Championship twice and delivering memorable matches against Kazuchika Okada and Shinsuke Nakamura. His success in Japan showcased his versatility and solidified his reputation as one of the best wrestlers in the world.

AJ's arrival in WWE in 2016 was a dream come true for his fans. He debuted at the Royal Rumble, receiving one of the loudest ovations in the event's history. AJ's WWE career quickly took off, as he feuded with stars like John Cena, Roman Reigns, and Daniel Bryan. His matches with Cena, particularly at SummerSlam 2016, are hailed as some of the best in WWE history.

In WWE, AJ became a two-time WWE Champion, with his first reign lasting an impressive 371 days. He also captured the Intercontinental, United States, and Tag Team Championships, proving his ability to excel in any role. His performances at WrestleMania, including a memorable match against The Undertaker in a cinematic Boneyard Match, cemented his legacy as one of WWE's top performers.

LEGENDS OF THE WRESTLING RING

Despite his success, AJ faced challenges throughout his career. Injuries and the demands of constant travel tested his physical and mental endurance. However, his faith and family kept him grounded. A devout Christian, AJ credits his faith for helping him navigate the highs and lows of his career. He is also a devoted husband to Wendy, his high school sweetheart, and a loving father to their four children.

Lesser-known facts about AJ include his passion for video games and his love for his hometown of Gainesville, Georgia, where he still resides. AJ is also known for his humility and generosity, often taking time to mentor younger wrestlers and engage with fans.

AJ Styles' story is one of perseverance, talent, and a relentless drive to be the best. From his humble beginnings in small-town Georgia to becoming a global wrestling icon, AJ's journey inspires countless fans and wrestlers alike. His ability to adapt, innovate, and connect with audiences makes him one of the most celebrated performers in wrestling history.

As of now, AJ Styles remains an active competitor in WWE, continuing to deliver phenomenal matches and moments. His legacy as "The Phenomenal One" is secure, proving that hard work, faith, and passion can lead to greatness in any arena.

25. Randy Orton: The Apex Predator

Randy Orton, born Randal Keith Orton on April 1, 1980, in Knoxville, Tennessee, is a third-generation professional wrestler whose name is synonymous with excellence in the wrestling world. Born into the legendary Orton wrestling family, Randy's father, "Cowboy" Bob Orton, and grandfather, Bob Orton Sr., were both celebrated wrestlers. Despite the family legacy, Randy's path to success was shaped by his unique charisma, unmatched talent, and relentless drive.

Growing up in St. Louis, Missouri, Randy showed an early interest in sports and adventure. However, his parents, Bob and Elaine Orton, were cautious about him pursuing wrestling, knowing the challenges of the industry. Randy attended Hazelwood Central High School, where he excelled in amateur wrestling but also displayed a rebellious streak that would later define his persona.

After high school, Randy enlisted in the United States Marine Corps but was discharged due to disciplinary issues. This experience became a turning point in his life, leading him to consider a career in professional wrestling. Randy began training at Ohio Valley Wrestling (OVW), WWE's developmental territory, where his natural talent and athleticism set him apart. He debuted in 2000, quickly catching the attention of WWE scouts.

Randy's WWE debut came in 2002 on SmackDown!, where he was introduced as a promising young talent. His early matches showcased his technical prowess and confidence, but his big break came when he joined Evolution, a dominant faction led by Triple H and Ric Flair. As the group's youngest member, Randy was groomed for greatness, and his nickname, "The Legend Killer," solidified his status as a rising star.

In 2004, at just 24 years old, Randy became the youngest World Heavyweight Champion in WWE history by defeating Chris Benoit at SummerSlam. This victory marked the beginning of his reign as one of WWE's top stars. Over the years, Randy's feuds with legends like The Undertaker, John Cena, and Triple H produced some of the most memorable moments in wrestling history.

Randy's finishing move, the RKO, became iconic, with its sudden execution and widespread popularity among fans. His rivalries often blurred the line between fiction and reality, particularly his intense battles with Edge, Seth Rollins, and Bray Wyatt. His ability to adapt to different storylines and opponents made him a versatile performer.

Throughout his career, Randy amassed an incredible list of achievements. He is a 14-time world champion, having held the WWE Championship and World Heavyweight Championship multiple times. He also won the Royal Rumble twice (2009 and 2017) and headlined several WrestleMania events. His accolades include the Money in the Bank briefcase and multiple Tag Team Championships, cementing his legacy as one of the greatest wrestlers of all time.

Despite his success, Randy faced challenges both inside and outside the ring. Early in his career, he struggled with anger issues and controversies, including suspensions for violating WWE's wellness policy. However, Randy used these setbacks as opportunities for growth, transforming into a respected locker room leader.

Lesser-known facts about Randy include his love for acting, with appearances in movies like 12 Rounds 2: Reloaded and The Condemned 2. He is also a devoted family man, often sharing glimpses of his life with his wife, Kim, and their children. Randy's ability to balance his intense wrestling persona with his personal life has earned him admiration from fans and peers alike.

One of Randy's most significant career moments came in 2020 when he feuded with Edge in a deeply personal storyline. Their Last Man Standing match at WrestleMania 36 showcased Randy's ability to deliver emotional, hard-hitting performances. This feud reminded fans of his longevity and adaptability in an ever-evolving industry.

As of now, Randy remains an active competitor in WWE, continuing to redefine his legacy. Known as "The Apex Predator," his calculated and ruthless in-ring style makes him a constant threat to any opponent. His longevity and ability to stay relevant in a highly competitive environment are testaments to his talent and work ethic.

Randy Orton's story is one of transformation and perseverance. From a rebellious youth to a wrestling legend, Randy's journey inspires fans to embrace their potential and overcome challenges. His legacy as one of the greatest performers in wrestling history is secure, with an RKO outta nowhere always waiting for his next opponent.

26. Roman Reigns: The Tribal Chief

Roman Reigns, born Leati Joseph Anoa'i on May 25, 1985, in Pensacola, Florida, is a wrestler who has redefined dominance in professional wrestling. A member of the legendary Anoa'i wrestling family, Roman is the son of Sika Anoa'i, a member of the iconic Wild Samoans tag team. His heritage, rich with wrestling royalty, includes relatives like Dwayne "The Rock" Johnson, Yokozuna, and Rikishi, ensuring that Roman's journey was steeped in legacy.

Growing up in Pensacola, Roman had an athletic childhood, excelling in football and other sports. His parents, Sika and Patricia, instilled values of discipline and hard work, guiding him to balance academics with his athletic pursuits. Roman attended Pensacola Catholic High School and later Escambia High School, where his performance on the football field earned him a scholarship to Georgia Institute of Technology. Playing as a defensive lineman for the Georgia Tech Yellow Jackets, Roman's leadership and skill stood out.

After graduating with a degree in management, Roman pursued professional football, signing with the Minnesota Vikings and later the Jacksonville Jaguars in 2007. Despite his talent, injuries, and circumstances cut short his football career. Determined not to let setbacks define him, Roman turned his attention to the family business—professional wrestling.

In 2010, Roman signed with WWE, training in their developmental territory, Florida Championship Wrestling (FCW). Wrestling under the name Roman Leakee, he showcased raw power and determination. His first official match wasn't a victory, but it was clear that Roman had the potential to make a significant impact.

Roman's big break came in 2012 when he debuted on WWE's main roster as part of The Shield, alongside Seth Rollins and Dean Ambrose. The Shield's rebellious, tactical persona captivated audiences, and their dominance in the ring established them as a force to be reckoned with. Roman's powerhouse role, coupled with his intense presence, made him a standout member of the group.

As a singles competitor, Roman's star continued to rise. In 2015, he won the Royal Rumble, securing his place in the WrestleMania main event against Brock Lesnar. Although he didn't win, the match showcased his resilience and star potential. Roman went on to win multiple championships, including the WWE World Heavyweight Championship and the Universal Championship, establishing himself as a top-tier performer.

One of the most significant turning points in Roman's career came in 2020 when he embraced his "Tribal Chief" persona. As the Head of the Table, Roman portrayed a dominant leader of his Samoan heritage, aligning with Paul Heyman and later feuding with his cousins, Jey and Jimmy Uso. This character transformation revitalized his career, earning widespread acclaim for its depth and authenticity.

Roman's achievements in WWE are extraordinary. He is a multi-time world champion, holding the Universal Championship for over 1,000 days—a record in the modern era. His rivalries with Brock Lesnar, John Cena, and Seth Rollins have delivered some of the most memorable matches in WWE history. Roman's finishing move, the Spear, has become iconic, often used to punctuate his dominance in the ring.

Despite his success, Roman faced significant challenges. In 2018, he shocked the world by revealing his battle with leukemia, forcing him to relinquish the Universal Championship. The announcement was a moment of vulnerability that deepened fans' connection to him. Roman's triumphant return in 2019 after successfully battling the disease further cemented his legacy as a fighter both inside and outside the ring.

Outside wrestling, Roman is a devoted family man. He is married to Galina Joelle Becker, his college sweetheart, and they have five children. Roman often speaks about the importance of family, a value reflected in his wrestling persona. He is also active in charity work, particularly with organizations focused on leukemia research and support.

Lesser-known facts about Roman include his passion for fitness and his role as an ambassador for various brands. He has also ventured into Hollywood, appearing in movies like Hobbs & Shaw alongside his cousin Dwayne Johnson.

As of now, Roman remains the centerpiece of WWE, delivering exceptional performances and redefining what it means to be a champion. His journey from a young football player to the Tribal Chief is a testament to resilience, adaptability, and a commitment to excellence.

Roman Reigns' legacy is still unfolding, but his impact on wrestling is undeniable. He has not only carried the torch of his family's legacy but has also blazed his own trail, becoming a global icon and an inspiration to millions. The Head of the Table will continue to dominate the squared circle, reminding everyone why he is the Tribal Chief.

27. Seth Rollins: The Visionary

Seth Rollins, born Colby Daniel Lopez on May 28, 1986, in Davenport, Iowa, is a wrestler whose blend of athleticism, charisma, and unpredictability has redefined modern professional wrestling. From humble beginnings to becoming a global superstar, Seth's story is one of determination, innovation, and an unyielding passion for his craft.

Growing up in the small town of Buffalo, Iowa, Colby was raised by his mother and stepfather. He adopted the last name Lopez from his stepfather, who was of Mexican descent. An introverted yet determined child, Colby found solace in sports and music, particularly punk rock. Attending Davenport West High School, he was a dedicated student and athlete, excelling in track and field. However, it was wrestling that truly captured his imagination. Inspired by legends like Shawn Michaels and Eddie Guerrero, he dreamed of stepping into the squared circle.

Colby began his wrestling journey in 2003, training at Danny Daniels' wrestling school in Chicago. Wrestling under the name "Tyler Black," he debuted in the independent circuit, performing for small crowds but showcasing immense potential. In 2007, he joined Ring of Honor (ROH), where he became a standout performer. His partnership with Jimmy Jacobs and their eventual feud displayed his versatility, while his reign as ROH World Champion solidified his status as a future star.

Seth's big break came in 2010 when he signed with WWE's developmental territory, Florida Championship Wrestling (FCW), which later became NXT. Rebranded as Seth Rollins, he quickly captured the attention of fans with his high-energy style and relatable persona. In 2012, Seth became the inaugural NXT Champion, a milestone that marked the beginning of his meteoric rise.

Seth's main roster debut came later that year as part of The Shield, alongside Roman Reigns and Dean Ambrose. The trio's tactical, rebellious approach took WWE by storm, dominating the tag team division and delivering unforgettable matches against teams like The Wyatt Family and Evolution. Seth's role as the group's architect highlighted his strategic mind and in-ring prowess.

The turning point in Seth's career came in 2014 when he betrayed The Shield, aligning himself with The Authority. The betrayal shocked fans but catapulted Seth into singles stardom. His run as Mr. Money in the Bank in 2014 showcased his cunning and opportunistic nature, culminating in a historic cash-in at WrestleMania 31. Seth's victory over Roman Reigns and Brock Lesnar to capture the WWE Championship is considered one of the greatest WrestleMania moments of all time.

Seth's achievements in WWE are remarkable. He is a multi-time WWE Champion, Universal Champion, and Grand Slam Champion, having won the Intercontinental, United States, and Tag Team Championships. His matches against stars like Finn Bálor, AJ Styles, and Cody Rhodes have been critically acclaimed, with his rivalry against Dean Ambrose (later Jon Moxley) being particularly personal and intense.

Despite his success, Seth faced significant challenges. A knee injury in 2015 sidelined him for months, forcing him to vacate the WWE Championship. The setback tested his resolve, but his triumphant return in 2016 at Extreme Rules reminded everyone of his resilience. Seth's adaptability also came to the forefront as he embraced multiple personas, from the sinister "Kingslayer" to the flamboyant "Visionary." Outside the ring, Seth is a devoted family man and entrepreneur. He married fellow WWE superstar Becky Lynch in 2021, and the couple welcomed their daughter, Roux, later that year. Seth also runs a wrestling academy in Davenport, Iowa, mentoring the next generation of talent. His love for video games and fitness reflects his dynamic personality, making him relatable to fans of all ages.

Lesser-known facts about Seth include his passion for coffee, which led him to open a coffee shop in his hometown. He is also known for his philanthropy, frequently supporting local charities and causes close to his heart.

As of now, Seth Rollins continues to be one of WWE's top stars, delivering show-stopping performances and redefining what it means to be a modern wrestler. His ability to connect with fans, both as a hero and a villain, ensures his legacy as one of the greatest performers of his generation.

Seth Rollins' journey from a small-town kid to a global icon is a testament to hard work, adaptability, and an unwavering belief in oneself. His story inspires fans to embrace their individuality, chase their dreams, and always strive to be "freakin' phenomenal."

28. Dean Ambrose: The Lunatic Fringe

Dean Ambrose, born Jonathan David Good on December 7, 1985, in Cincinnati, Ohio, is a wrestler whose wild, unfiltered persona made him a fan favorite in the world of professional wrestling. Growing up in the rough neighborhoods of Cincinnati, Jon's early life was marked by hardship. Raised in a single-parent household with his mother, he faced financial struggles and lived in a dangerous environment. Wrestling became his escape, offering him a glimpse of a life beyond his tough upbringing.

Jon's fascination with wrestling began as a teenager. He idolized stars like Bret Hart and Stone Cold Steve Austin, immersing himself in wrestling tapes and magazines. The sport's larger-than-life personas and gritty storytelling resonated deeply with him, igniting a passion that would drive him to pursue wrestling as a career. He dropped out of high school to chase his dream, dedicating himself entirely to the craft.

Jon began his wrestling career in 2004 on the independent circuit, wrestling under the ring name "Jon Moxley." He trained under Les Thatcher and worked in the Heartland Wrestling Association (HWA), where his unrelenting work ethic and willingness to take risks set him apart. His hardcore style, which included violent matches involving barbed wire and thumbtacks, quickly earned him a cult following.

In 2011, Jon signed with WWE and adopted the name Dean Ambrose. He started in their developmental territory, Florida Championship Wrestling (FCW), later rebranded as NXT. Dean's intensity and charisma caught the attention of WWE management, paving the way for his debut on the main roster.

Dean's WWE debut came in 2012 as a member of The Shield, alongside Seth Rollins and Roman Reigns. The Shield's rebellious, tactical persona shook WWE to its core, and Dean's role as the group's unhinged wildcard made him a standout. The trio dominated the tag team division and delivered classic matches against top factions like Evolution and The Wyatt Family.

After The Shield disbanded in 2014, Dean embarked on a successful singles career. His feud with Seth Rollins was one of WWE's most compelling storylines, fueled by betrayal and personal animosity. Dean's unpredictable, no-holds-barred style made him a fan favorite, earning him the nickname "The Lunatic Fringe."

Dean's accomplishments in WWE include holding the WWE Championship, Intercontinental Championship, United States Championship, and Tag Team Championships. He is one of the few wrestlers to achieve the Grand Slam, winning all major WWE titles. His cash-in of the Money in the Bank contract in 2016 to defeat Seth Rollins for the WWE Championship remains a highlight of his career.

Despite his success, Dean faced challenges. Injuries, including a triceps injury in 2017 that sidelined him for months, tested his resilience. He also struggled with WWE's creative direction, often feeling his character was stifled by scripted storylines. These frustrations eventually led to his departure from WWE in 2019.

After leaving WWE, Jon revived his Jon Moxley persona and joined All Elite Wrestling (AEW). His debut at AEW's Double or Nothing event was explosive, signaling a new chapter in his career. Jon quickly established himself as a top star, capturing the AEW World Championship in 2020. His brutal, hard-hitting matches against Kenny Omega, Chris Jericho, and Eddie Kingston showcased his ability to thrive in a less-restrictive environment.

Lesser-known facts about Jon include his passion for reading and his love for animals, particularly his rescue dog. He is married to Renee Paquette, a former WWE broadcaster, and the couple welcomed their first child, Nora, in 2021. Jon is known for his humility and down-to-earth demeanor, often shying away from the limelight outside the ring.

Jon's willingness to push boundaries and embrace chaos has made him one of wrestling's most compelling performers. His journey from a troubled teenager in Cincinnati to a global wrestling icon is a testament to the power of grit and perseverance.

As of now, Jon Moxley remains one of AEW's top stars, continuing to deliver electrifying performances. His legacy as Dean Ambrose in WWE and Jon Moxley in AEW cements his place as one of wrestling's most versatile and enduring characters. The Lunatic Fringe's story reminds fans that success comes not just from talent but from the courage to be unapologetically yourself.

29. Batista: The Animal Unleashed

Batista, born David Michael Bautista Jr. on January 18, 1969, in Washington, D.C., is a wrestler who rose from a challenging upbringing to become one of the most dominant and charismatic stars in WWE history. Known for his powerhouse style and larger-than-life persona, Batista's journey is a tale of resilience, transformation, and relentless pursuit of greatness.

David grew up in a tough neighborhood in Arlington, Virginia. His parents, Donna Raye and David Bautista Sr. separated when he was young. Raised primarily by his mother, David witnessed the harsh realities of life early on. By the age of nine, he had already experienced poverty and violence in his community, which shaped his drive to overcome adversity. Despite these challenges, he found solace in bodybuilding and martial arts, channeling his frustrations into physical pursuits.

David attended Wakefield High School but struggled academically, leaving school to work odd jobs, including as a nightclub bouncer and a lifeguard. His imposing physique and work ethic eventually led him to professional bodybuilding. However, he longed for something more fulfilling, and the spark for wrestling ignited when he attended a live WWE event.

Batista's wrestling journey began in 1999 when he joined the Wild Samoan Training Center, operated by WWE legend Afa Anoaʻi. Under Afa's guidance, Batista honed his skills and debuted in Ohio Valley Wrestling (OVW), WWE's developmental territory, as Leviathan. His raw power and menacing persona caught WWE's attention, and he signed with the company in 2000.

Batista made his WWE main roster debut in 2002 as "Deacon Batista," a bodyguard for Reverend D-Von. While the gimmick was short-lived, it showcased his potential. The real breakthrough came when he joined Evolution, a dominant faction led by Triple H, Ric Flair, and Randy Orton. As Evolution's enforcer, Batista gained invaluable experience and developed his character as a ruthless powerhouse.

In 2005, Batista broke away from Evolution, turning on Triple H to forge his own path. His victory over Triple H at WrestleMania 21 to capture the World Heavyweight Championship marked the beginning of his reign as a top star. Batista's intense matches against The Undertaker, John Cena, and Edge further solidified his status as a main-event performer.

Batista's accolades in WWE are staggering. He is a six-time world champion, a four-time Tag Team Champion, and the winner of two Royal Rumble matches (2005 and 2014). His finishing move, the Batista Bomb, became a symbol of his dominance, often leaving opponents flattened in his wake.

Despite his success, Batista's career was not without challenges. Injuries plagued him throughout his wrestling journey, including a torn triceps that sidelined him for months. Additionally, he faced criticism from some fans and peers for his meteoric rise, but Batista silenced doubters with his dedication and consistent performances.

One of Batista's most significant career moments came in 2014 when he returned to WWE after a four-year hiatus. Though his return initially received mixed reactions, Batista embraced the fan backlash, turning it into a compelling storyline. His final match at WrestleMania 35 in 2019, a brutal No Holds Barred bout against Triple H, was a fitting end to his wrestling career, showcasing the intensity and emotion that defined his journey.

Outside wrestling, Batista has made a successful transition to Hollywood, becoming a global movie star. His breakout role as Drax the Destroyer in Marvel's Guardians of the Galaxy showcased his comedic timing and acting range, earning him critical acclaim. He has also appeared in films like Spectre, Blade Runner 2049, and Army of the Dead, proving his versatility as an actor.

Lesser-known facts about Batista include his love for tattoos, with his collection reflecting his life's journey and personal beliefs. He is also a passionate advocate for animal rights, often supporting organizations dedicated to animal welfare.

Batista's personal life has seen its share of ups and downs. He has been married three times and is a devoted father to his two daughters. Despite his fame, Batista remains grounded, often crediting his humble beginnings for keeping him focused on his goals.

Batista's story is one of transformation and perseverance. From a troubled youth in Washington, D.C., to a WWE Hall of Famer and Hollywood star, he has continually reinvented himself, proving that hard work and resilience can overcome any obstacle.

As of now, Batista enjoys his retirement from wrestling, focusing on his acting career and personal passions. His legacy as "The Animal" in WWE and as a respected actor in Hollywood ensures that his name will be remembered for generations. David Bautista's journey reminds us all to embrace challenges, pursue dreams relentlessly, and never underestimate the power of transformation.

30. Drew McIntyre: The Scottish Warrior

Drew McIntyre, born Andrew McLean Galloway IV on June 6, 1985, in Ayr, Scotland, is a professional wrestler who overcame challenges and setbacks to become one of WWE's most inspirational stars. His journey from a small town in Scotland to the global stage of WWE is a tale of determination, resilience, and triumph.

Drew grew up in Prestwick, a coastal town in Scotland, with his parents, Angela and Andrew Galloway. From an early age, he was drawn to sports and physical activities, showing a natural athleticism. Inspired by wrestling icons like Bret Hart and Shawn Michaels, Drew began dreaming of a career in professional wrestling. His parents supported his passion, even though wrestling was not as prominent in Scotland as in the United States.

Drew attended Prestwick Academy and later studied criminology at Glasgow Caledonian University, balancing his studies with his burgeoning wrestling ambitions. At 15, he began training with the British Championship Wrestling (BCW) promotion in Scotland. Drew's early matches displayed his raw potential and relentless work ethic, setting him apart in the local wrestling scene.

In 2006, Drew signed with WWE, becoming the first Scotsman to join the company. He debuted on the main roster in 2007 but struggled to make an impact initially. Drew returned to WWE's developmental territories, where he refined his skills and adopted the name Drew McIntyre. In 2009, Drew re-debuted on SmackDown! as "The Chosen One," handpicked by WWE Chairman Vince McMahon as a future world champion. His early success included winning the Intercontinental Championship and the Tag Team Championship with Cody Rhodes.

However, Drew's career took a downturn in the mid-2010s. A series of injuries and inconsistent booking led to him being relegated to comedic roles as part of the 3MB faction. In 2014, Drew was released from WWE, a moment that could have ended his career. Instead, it became a turning point.

Determined to rebuild himself, Drew returned to the independent circuit, wrestling for promotions like Insane Championship Wrestling (ICW), Evolve, and Impact Wrestling. He transformed his physique, honed his craft, and developed a more intense and commanding persona. Drew's work during this period earned him respect from fans and peers alike, proving his worth as a top-tier talent.

In 2017, Drew returned to WWE, debuting in NXT. His performances were electrifying, and he captured the NXT Championship, marking his resurgence. Drew's transition to WWE's main roster in 2018 was equally impactful. His rivalries with Roman Reigns, Seth Rollins, and Dolph Ziggler showcased his growth as a performer.

Drew's defining moment came at the 2020 Royal Rumble, where he eliminated Brock Lesnar and won the match. This victory earned him a shot at the WWE Championship at WrestleMania 36. Despite the challenges of performing during the COVID-19 pandemic, Drew defeated Lesnar to win his first WWE Championship, fulfilling the prophecy of "The Chosen One."

LEGENDS OF THE WRESTLING RING

As WWE Champion, Drew carried the company through difficult times, delivering stellar matches and embodying the spirit of a resilient champion. His Claymore Kick finishing move became one of the most feared in wrestling, and his Scottish warrior persona resonated with fans worldwide.

Drew's journey was not without personal challenges. The loss of his mother in 2012 deeply affected him, but her memory continues to inspire him. Drew's ability to overcome setbacks and emerge stronger is a testament to his character.

Outside the ring, Drew is a devoted husband to Kaitlyn Frohnapfel, whom he married in 2016. He is also a passionate ambassador for wrestling, frequently engaging with fans and promoting the sport in his native Scotland and beyond.

Lesser-known facts about Drew include his love for heavy metal music and his childhood dream of becoming a football player. He is also a published author, with his autobiography A Chosen Destiny detailing his life and career.

As of now, Drew remains one of WWE's top stars, inspiring millions with his story of redemption and perseverance. His legacy as the first Scotsman to win the WWE Championship and his contributions to wrestling make him a role model for aspiring wrestlers worldwide.

Drew McIntyre's journey is a testament to the power of resilience and self-belief. From the small town of Prestwick to the grandest stages of wrestling, Drew's story reminds us that even in the face of setbacks, greatness is achievable with hard work and determination.

31. Finn Bálor: The Demon King

Finn Bálor, born Fergal Devitt on July 25, 1981, in Bray, County Wicklow, Ireland, is a professional wrestler whose creativity, athleticism, and charisma have captivated fans worldwide. Known for his enigmatic persona and theatrical entrances, Finn's journey from a small town in Ireland to the global stage of WWE is a testament to his dedication and talent.

Fergal grew up in a close-knit family with his parents and three siblings. From a young age, he displayed a passion for sports, particularly soccer and Gaelic football. However, it was wrestling that truly captured his imagination. Watching icons like Shawn Michaels and The British Bulldog inspired him to pursue his dream of stepping into the squared circle. Encouraged by his parents, Fergal began his journey into professional wrestling.

After completing his education at St. Brendan's College in Bray, Fergal sought out training opportunities. He joined NWA UK Hammerlock, a respected wrestling school in the United Kingdom, where he honed his skills under the guidance of seasoned trainers. His natural talent

LEGENDS OF THE WRESTLING RING

and determination quickly set him apart, and he made his professional debut in 2001 at the age of 20.

Wrestling under his real name, Fergal Devitt, he gained recognition on the European and Japanese circuits. In 2006, he moved to Japan and joined New Japan Pro-Wrestling (NJPW), where he adopted the ring name "Prince Devitt." His career in NJPW was transformative, as he developed his signature high-flying style and honed his storytelling abilities. Devitt's rivalry with stars like Hiroshi Tanahashi and his leadership of the Bullet Club faction elevated him to international stardom.

During his time in NJPW, Finn captured the IWGP Junior Heavyweight Championship three times and won the Best of the Super Juniors tournament twice. His innovative matches and theatrical entrances, including his occasional transformation into the "Demon King," a darker, more intense version of himself, became fan favorites.

In 2014, Finn signed with WWE and adopted the name Finn Bálor, a nod to Irish mythology and his heritage. "Finn" derives from Fionn mac Cumhaill, a legendary Irish hero, while "Bálor" references Balor, a mythical demon king. His WWE debut in NXT marked the beginning of a new chapter. Finn quickly became the face of the brand, capturing the NXT Championship and delivering unforgettable matches against stars like Kevin Owens and Samoa Joe.

Finn's success in NXT led to his promotion to WWE's main roster in 2016. He made an immediate impact, becoming the first-ever Universal Champion at SummerSlam by defeating Seth Rollins. However, tragedy struck during the match, as Finn suffered a severe shoulder injury that forced him to relinquish the title the next night. This setback tested his resilience, but Finn returned stronger, earning the admiration of fans for his determination.

Despite facing challenges, including injuries and inconsistent booking, Finn remained a fan favorite. His rivalries with stars like Bray Wyatt, Roman Reigns, and AJ Styles showcased his versatility and ability to adapt to different storylines. His transformation into the "Demon King" during major matches became a signature element, adding an extra layer of drama to his performances.

Outside the ring, Finn is known for his humility and creativity. He is an avid artist and a passionate advocate for mental health awareness, often using his platform to inspire others. Finn is also a devoted family man and married Veronica Rodriguez, a Fox Sports presenter, in 2019.

Lesser-known facts about Finn include his love for Lego and his background in martial arts. He holds a black belt in kickboxing, which adds a unique flair to his wrestling style. Finn's ability to connect with fans, both as a hero and a villain, is a testament to his charisma and authenticity.

As of now, Finn continues to be a prominent figure in WWE, representing both the SmackDown and Raw brands. His legacy as an innovator and a performer who pushes boundaries ensures his place among wrestling's elite.

Finn Bálor's story is one of passion, perseverance, and creativity. From his beginnings in a small Irish town to becoming a global wrestling icon, Finn's journey inspires fans to embrace their uniqueness and chase their dreams. The Demon King's legacy is one of excellence, reminding us that greatness comes from both talent and heart.

32. Kofi Kingston: The Ghanaian Sensation

Kofi Kingston, born Kofi Nahaje Sarkodie-Mensah on August 14, 1981, in Kumasi, Ghana, is a wrestler who captivated audiences with his electrifying moves and vibrant personality. Kofi's journey from West Africa to becoming a WWE Champion is a story of determination, creativity, and an unrelenting spirit.

Kofi spent his early childhood in Kumasi, Ghana, surrounded by a loving family that valued education and hard work. His parents, Kwasi and Elizabeth Sarkodie-Mensah decided to move the family to the United States when Kofi was a young boy, seeking better opportunities. They settled in the Boston area, where Kofi adapted to a new culture while maintaining pride in his Ghanaian roots.

Kofi attended Winchester High School in Massachusetts, excelling academically and athletically. He later pursued a degree in communications at Boston College, preparing for a career outside of sports. However, his love for wrestling, inspired by watching WWE legends like Shawn Michaels and Ricky Steamboat, kept growing. He realized that his true calling lay inside the squared circle.

After college, Kofi decided to pursue his wrestling dreams. He trained at Chaotic Wrestling, a local promotion in New England, where he began honing his skills. Kofi's athleticism, combined with his infectious charisma, set him apart. Wrestling under his real name and later adopting the ring name "Kofi Kingston," he quickly gained recognition on the independent circuit.

Kofi's big break came in 2007 when he signed with WWE. He debuted in the developmental territory Florida Championship Wrestling (FCW), where he embraced his Ghanaian heritage, adopting a Jamaican-inspired persona to emphasize his unique identity. His infectious energy and high-flying moves made him a standout, and he soon debuted on WWE's main roster in 2008.

Kofi's main roster debut on ECW showcased his talent, and he quickly became a fan favorite. His positivity and acrobatic style were a breath of fresh air. In his first year, Kofi captured the Intercontinental Championship, proving he was more than just an entertainer—he was a legitimate competitor.

Throughout his career, Kofi achieved numerous accolades. He is a four-time Intercontinental Champion, a three-time United States Champion, and an impressive 15-time Tag Team Champion. As part of The New Day, alongside Xavier Woods and Big E, Kofi redefined tag team wrestling. Their combination of humor, athleticism, and camaraderie made them one of the most successful and beloved factions in WWE history.

Kofi's defining moment came in 2019, during the "KofiMania" storyline. After years of being a reliable mid-card talent, Kofi's perseverance paid off. Fans rallied behind him as he earned a WWE Championship match at WrestleMania 35 against Daniel Bryan. In an emotional and hard-fought battle, Kofi defeated Bryan to become the first African-born WWE Champion. The victory was a watershed moment, celebrating representation and inspiring fans around the world.

Kofi's career was not without challenges. Early on, he faced stereotypes and had to fight to be taken seriously in a company dominated by larger-than-life personas. Injuries and setbacks tested his resolve, but Kofi's unwavering positivity kept him moving forward.

Lesser-known facts about Kofi include his love for video games, which he shares with his New Day teammates on their popular YouTube channel, UpUpDownDown. He is also an avid comic book fan and often incorporates superhero themes into his wrestling gear. Kofi's creative approach to his craft is exemplified by his innovative performances in the Royal Rumble, where his gravity-defying escapes have become legendary.

Outside the ring, Kofi is a devoted husband and father of three. He often speaks about the importance of family and credits his wife, Kori, for supporting him throughout his journey. Kofi also gives back to the community, frequently participating in WWE's charitable initiatives and advocating for children's education.

As of now, Kofi remains an active competitor, continuing to entertain fans with his boundless energy and skill. His legacy as a trailblazer and role model is secure, inspiring countless people to chase their dreams regardless of the odds.

Kofi Kingston's story is one of perseverance, joy, and the power of believing in oneself. From a small boy in Ghana to a global WWE superstar, Kofi's journey is a reminder that with hard work and a positive attitude, anything is possible. KofiMania lives on, proving that sometimes, the good guys really do win.

33. Big E: The Powerhouse of Positivity

Big E, born Ettore Ewen on March 1, 1986, in Tampa, Florida, is a professional wrestler whose infectious charisma and incredible strength have made him one of WWE's most beloved superstars. From his athletic roots to becoming a WWE Champion, Big E's journey is a testament to hard work, perseverance, and the power of positivity.

Ettore grew up in Tampa, Florida, in a supportive household with his parents, Ettore and Margaret Ewen. His parents, originally from Jamaica and Montserrat, instilled in him a strong sense of discipline and family values. As a child, Ettore was quiet but competitive, excelling in both academics and sports. He attended Wharton High School, where he shone as a football player and wrestler, earning accolades for his strength and athleticism.

After high school, Ettore attended the University of Iowa on a football scholarship, playing as a defensive lineman for the Hawkeyes. His college football career was promising, but injuries cut his aspirations short. Determined not to let setbacks define him, Ettore turned to powerlifting, where he found tremendous success. He became a champion powerlifter, setting state and national records, and earning recognition for his incredible strength.

Ettore's transition into professional wrestling came in 2009 when he signed with WWE's developmental territory, Florida Championship Wrestling (FCW). Adopting the ring name "Big E Langston," he quickly made an impression with his raw power and explosive energy. His debut match in FCW showcased his potential, and he soon became one of the promotion's standout performers.

Big E's WWE main roster debut came in 2012 when he aligned with Dolph Ziggler and AJ Lee as an enforcer. While this role highlighted his physical dominance, it was his alliance with Kofi Kingston and Xavier Woods in 2014 that transformed his career. Together, they formed The New Day, a faction that combined humor, athleticism, and positivity to win over fans worldwide.

The New Day's success was unprecedented. The trio became one of the most decorated tag teams in WWE history, winning 12 Tag Team Championships and holding the record for the longest reign at 483 days. Big E's larger-than-life personality and unique moves, like the Big Ending and his explosive Spear, made him a fan favorite.

In 2021, Big E embarked on a singles career, capturing the Money in the Bank briefcase and cashing it in to win the WWE Championship. His victory was a deeply emotional moment, not just for Big E but for fans who had followed his journey. As champion, Big E represented resilience, joy, and inclusivity, becoming a role model for fans of all ages.

Despite his success, Big E faced challenges throughout his career. Injuries, including a serious neck injury in 2022, tested his resolve. However, his positive attitude and strong support system helped him overcome these setbacks. Big E's ability to stay optimistic and connect with fans on a personal level has been a hallmark of his career.

Outside the ring, Big E is known for his humor, generosity, and love for entertainment. He is a founding member of UpUpDownDown, a gaming YouTube channel, and has voiced his passion for anime, video games, and comic books. Big E also takes pride in his Jamaican heritage, often incorporating elements of his culture into his persona.

Lesser-known facts about Big E include his love for motivational speaking and his involvement in charitable work, particularly for children's health and education initiatives. He is deeply committed to making a positive impact beyond wrestling, using his platform to inspire and uplift others.

As of now, Big E remains a vital part of WWE, whether competing in the ring or representing the company in various capacities. His story is a reminder that strength is not just physical but also mental and emotional. Big E's journey from a quiet child in Tampa to a WWE Champion is proof that hard work, resilience, and positivity can overcome any obstacle.

Big E's legacy is one of joy, resilience, and the unyielding belief in the power of positivity. His journey inspires millions, proving that greatness is achieved not just through strength but through heart and determination. The New Day's creed—"New Day Rocks!"—is not just a chant but a celebration of life, love, and the endless possibilities of what we can achieve together.

34. Xavier Woods: The Maestro of Positivity

Xavier Woods, born Austin Watson on September 4, 1986, in Columbus, Georgia, is a wrestler whose energy, charisma, and creativity have made him one of WWE's most unique stars. A member of The New Day, Xavier's journey is a blend of intellectual curiosity, athletic prowess, and an unyielding passion for entertaining others.

Austin grew up in a loving household with parents who valued education and hard work. As a child, he was a bundle of energy, exploring various interests, from music and academics to video games and sports. His parents encouraged his curiosity, fostering a love for learning that would define his life. Xavier attended Sprayberry High School, where he excelled academically and athletically, particularly in wrestling and track.

After high school, Austin pursued higher education, earning a bachelor's degree in psychology from Furman University. His interest in the human mind complemented his physical talents, giving him a deeper understanding of discipline and motivation. He didn't stop there—Austin later earned a master's degree in psychology, setting himself apart as one of WWE's most educated performers.

Austin's path to wrestling began with a childhood love for the sport. Inspired by legends like Ric Flair and Shawn Michaels, he dreamed of stepping into the ring. After completing his education, Austin trained in professional wrestling while balancing his academic pursuits. His early wrestling career saw him perform under the ring name "Consequences Creed" in Total Nonstop Action Wrestling (TNA), where he quickly gained a reputation for his high-energy style and entertaining personality.

In 2010, Austin signed with WWE, adopting the ring name Xavier Woods. He began in Florida Championship Wrestling (FCW), WWE's developmental territory, before debuting on the main roster in 2013. Initially, Xavier struggled to find his footing, but his fortunes changed in 2014 when he teamed up with Big E and Kofi Kingston to form The New Day.

The New Day's rise to prominence was meteoric. Combining humor, positivity, and unmatched chemistry, the trio redefined tag team wrestling. Their creative promos, vibrant attire, and in-ring excellence endeared them to fans worldwide. Xavier's trombone, affectionately named "Francesca," became a signature part of their act, adding a unique musical flair to their performances.

The New Day's success is unparalleled. They have won 12 Tag Team Championships, including the longest reign in WWE history at 483 days. Xavier's contributions, both in and out of the ring, have been instrumental in their success. His comedic timing, quick wit, and innovative wrestling style have made him a fan favorite.

Despite his success, Xavier has faced challenges. Injuries, including a torn Achilles tendon in 2019, tested his resilience. However, his determination to overcome setbacks and his ability to adapt kept him moving forward. Xavier's passion for connecting with fans and spreading positivity has been a driving force throughout his career.

LEGENDS OF THE WRESTLING RING

Lesser-known facts about Xavier include his love for video games and his role as the founder of the popular YouTube gaming channel UpUpDownDown. The channel showcases Xavier's gaming skills and personality, earning a loyal following among wrestling and gaming fans alike. He is also a talented musician, often incorporating his musical abilities into his wrestling persona.

Outside the ring, Xavier is a devoted husband and father. He frequently speaks about the importance of family and values the support of his wife, Jess, and their children. Xavier is also an advocate for education, often encouraging young fans to pursue their dreams while emphasizing the importance of learning.

Xavier's versatility extends beyond wrestling. He has appeared on various television shows, collaborated with musicians, and spoken at events about the power of positivity and perseverance. His ability to connect with people from all walks of life makes him a true ambassador for WWE.

As of now, Xavier continues to entertain fans as part of The New Day while pursuing new ventures in gaming, music, and education. His legacy as a wrestler, entertainer, and role model is secure, inspiring countless fans to embrace their individuality and chase their dreams.

Xavier Woods' story is one of passion, perseverance, and joy. From a curious child in Columbus, Georgia, to a global WWE superstar, Xavier's journey reminds us that with determination, creativity, and a positive outlook, anything is possible. The power of positivity is more than a slogan—it's a way of life that Xavier embodies every day.

35. Chris Benoit: The Wrestling Technician

Chris Benoit, born on May 21, 1967, in Montreal, Quebec, Canada, was one of the most technically gifted professional wrestlers of his generation. Known as "The Rabid Wolverine" and "The Canadian Crippler," Benoit's career was marked by his unparalleled dedication to the craft of wrestling. Despite the tragic and controversial end to his life, his professional accomplishments showcased his passion and discipline within the squared circle.

Chris spent his early years in Edmonton, Alberta, where he was raised by his parents, Michael and Margaret Benoit. As a child, he was inspired by wrestling legends like the Dynamite Kid and Bret Hart, watching them on television and attending live events at the Calgary Stampede Wrestling promotion. It was in these formative years that Benoit decided to pursue a career in professional wrestling.

After graduating from Archbishop O'Leary Catholic High School, Benoit trained at the famous Hart Dungeon under the guidance of Stu Hart, a revered figure in wrestling. The rigorous training in Calgary shaped Benoit into a disciplined and highly skilled wrestler. His early exposure to the technical and physical demands of the sport laid the foundation for his success.

Benoit made his professional debut in 1985 with Stampede Wrestling, where he adopted a style that emphasized technical precision and intensity. His first major match, though unremarkable in outcome, demonstrated his potential and garnered attention from wrestling promoters. Over the next few years, Benoit honed his craft in Japan, joining New Japan Pro-Wrestling (NJPW) and competing as "Wild Pegasus." His tenure in NJPW saw him win the prestigious Best of the Super Juniors tournament in 1993 and 1995, establishing him as one of the premier junior heavyweights in the world.

In the mid-1990s, Benoit joined Extreme Championship Wrestling (ECW) in the United States. His time in ECW was brief but impactful, as he engaged in memorable matches and earned the nickname "The Canadian Crippler" after an unfortunate incident where a botched move injured another wrestler. This period further solidified his reputation as a fearless and technical performer.

Benoit's career took a major turn when he signed with World Championship Wrestling (WCW) in 1995. In WCW, Benoit joined the legendary Four Horsemen stable and engaged in high-profile rivalries. Despite his undeniable talent, Benoit struggled to break into the main event scene due to backstage politics and inconsistent booking. However, he won the WCW World Heavyweight Championship in 2000, though he left the company shortly after due to frustrations with management.

In 2000, Benoit joined the World Wrestling Federation (WWF, later WWE). His WWE debut as part of The Radicalz—a group of wrestlers who transitioned from WCW—marked the beginning of his rise to global stardom. Benoit quickly became a mainstay in WWE's mid-card and main event scenes, capturing the Intercontinental Championship, and Tag Team Championships, and engaging in classic matches with stars like Kurt Angle, Chris Jericho, and Eddie Guerrero.

One of Benoit's career-defining moments came at WrestleMania XX in 2004, where he defeated Triple H and Shawn Michaels in a triple-threat match to win the World Heavyweight Championship. The emotional celebration with his close friend Eddie Guerrero, who also held the WWE Championship at the time, remains one of the most iconic moments in wrestling history.

Benoit's achievements include winning multiple world championships, intercontinental titles, and tag team championships across various promotions. His technical ability, intensity, and commitment to his craft earned him the respect of fans and peers alike.

Despite his professional success, Benoit faced challenges in his personal life. His rigorous schedule and physical style took a toll on his body and mental health. Tragically, his life ended in June 2007 under circumstances that shocked the wrestling world. The events surrounding his death cast a shadow over his legacy, prompting debates about the effects of head injuries and mental health in professional wrestling.

Chris Benoit's legacy in wrestling is complex. While his in-ring accomplishments remain a testament to his skill and dedication, the circumstances of his death have led to his career being largely excluded from official WWE history. Nonetheless, fans and wrestlers who knew him remember his passion for wrestling and the impact he had on the industry.

Benoit's story is a cautionary tale that underscores the importance of addressing mental health and the physical toll of professional sports. His career serves as a reminder of the heights that dedication can achieve and the need for compassion and awareness in the face of personal struggles.

36. Davey Boy Smith: The British Bulldog

Davey Boy Smith, famously known as "The British Bulldog," was a wrestler who left an indelible mark on the world of professional wrestling with his charisma, strength, and in-ring prowess. Born on November 27, 1962, in Golborne, Lancashire, England, Davey grew up in a working-class family, embodying the grit and determination that would define his career.

Davey's childhood was modest, filled with the simple joys of life in a small English town. He was raised alongside his siblings by hardworking parents who instilled in him the values of perseverance and discipline. As a young boy, he was drawn to sports, particularly soccer and wrestling, showcasing a natural athletic ability that hinted at his future.

His love for wrestling was ignited by watching matches on television and attending live events in his area. At the age of 15, Davey began training under Ted Betley, a respected local wrestling coach. His cousin, Tom Billington, better known as the Dynamite Kid, also trained under Betley, and the two formed a bond that would lead to their eventual tag team success.

Davey made his wrestling debut in the United Kingdom, where his combination of strength and agility quickly made him a standout. In the late 1970s, he joined forces with Dynamite Kid, and the duo gained recognition in Japan and North America. Their tag team, known as The British Bulldogs, became one of the most innovative and exciting pairs in professional wrestling.

The British Bulldogs gained prominence in Stampede Wrestling, a Canadian promotion owned by the legendary Hart family. It was here that Davey met Diana Hart, whom he would later marry, further cementing his ties to wrestling royalty. The Bulldogs' matches in Stampede showcased their groundbreaking style, blending high-flying maneuvers with power moves, captivating audiences and earning them a contract with WWE (then WWF) in 1984.

In WWE, The British Bulldogs became fan favorites, known for their dynamic chemistry and iconic mascot, Matilda the bulldog. Their crowning achievement came at WrestleMania 2 in 1986 when they defeated The Dream Team (Greg Valentine and Brutus Beefcake) to win the WWE Tag Team Championship. The victory solidified their place as one of the greatest tag teams of their era.

Despite their success, the partnership between Davey and Dynamite Kid eventually dissolved due to personal and professional differences. Davey transitioned into a singles career, adopting the moniker "The British Bulldog." His solo journey was marked by numerous accolades, including memorable feuds with stars like Bret Hart, Shawn Michaels, and Vader.

One of Davey's most iconic moments came at SummerSlam 1992, held at Wembley Stadium in London. In front of a hometown crowd of over 80,000 fans, Davey defeated Bret Hart to win the Intercontinental Championship. The match is widely regarded as one of the greatest in WWE history, showcasing Davey's technical skill and the emotional connection he had with fans.

Davey's career was not without challenges. Injuries and personal struggles, including issues with substance abuse, affected his performance and relationships within the industry. Despite these setbacks, Davey remained a beloved figure among fans, known for his resilience and dedication to wrestling.

Lesser-known facts about Davey include his passion for bodybuilding and his role as a mentor to younger wrestlers. He was deeply committed to his craft, often training rigorously to maintain his physique and enhance his in-ring abilities. Davey's influence extended beyond the ring, as he inspired a generation of British wrestlers to pursue their dreams on the global stage.

In the late 1990s, Davey returned to WWE for a final run, achieving moderate success. However, injuries and personal issues led to his retirement from active competition in 2000. Davey spent his post-wrestling years focusing on his family and health, but his life was tragically cut short. On May 18, 2002, Davey Boy Smith passed away from a heart attack while on vacation in British Columbia, Canada. He was 39 years old.

Davey's legacy in wrestling is profound. He was posthumously inducted into the WWE Hall of Fame in 2020, an honor that celebrated his contributions to the sport and his enduring impact on fans worldwide. His son, Harry Smith (also known as Davey Boy Smith Jr.), has followed in his footsteps, carrying on the family legacy in professional wrestling.

Davey Boy Smith's story is one of triumph, challenges, and inspiration. From his humble beginnings in Lancashire to becoming a global wrestling icon, Davey's journey reflects the power of determination and passion. The British Bulldog remains a symbol of strength, resilience, and the enduring spirit of wrestling.

37. Andre the Giant: The Eighth Wonder of the World

Andre the Giant, born André René Roussimoff on May 19, 1946, in Coulommiers, France, was a wrestler whose incredible size, strength, and charisma made him a cultural icon. Standing at 7 feet 4 inches tall and weighing over 500 pounds, Andre was aptly nicknamed "The Eighth Wonder of the World." His story is one of remarkable achievements, physical challenges, and an enduring legacy.

Andre was born into a farming family in the small village of Molien, near Coulommiers. His parents, Boris and Mariann Roussimoff were of Bulgarian and Polish descent, and they raised their five children with strong values of hard work and humility. Andre's size became apparent early in life, and by the time he was 12, he was already over 6 feet tall. He suffered from acromegaly, a rare hormonal disorder caused by excess growth hormone, which contributed to his extraordinary stature.

Despite his physical challenges, Andre was a bright and curious child. He excelled in school but left at the age of 14 to work on his family's farm. His immense size and strength made him well-suited for labor, but he dreamed of a life beyond the fields. A chance encounter with French wrestling promoter Édouard Carpentier introduced Andre to the world of professional wrestling.

Andre began training under Carpentier and made his wrestling debut in 1964. Wrestling under various names, including "Géant Ferré," he quickly gained popularity in France and neighboring countries. His size and agility for someone of his stature set him apart, and he was soon touring Japan, where he gained international fame.

In the 1970s, Andre joined the American wrestling circuit, where he adopted the moniker "Andre the Giant." He became a global sensation, competing in territories across the United States, Canada, and beyond. Andre's matches were spectacles, as fans marveled at his size and strength. He often faced multiple opponents at once, defeating them with ease, further cementing his legend.

Andre's career reached new heights when he joined the World Wrestling Federation (WWF, now WWE) in 1973. Under the management of Vince McMahon Sr., Andre became one of the company's biggest draws. His undefeated streak lasted for nearly 15 years, and his battles with stars like Big John Studd, Harley Race, and Hulk Hogan became the stuff of wrestling lore.

One of Andre's most iconic moments came at WrestleMania III in 1987, where he faced Hulk Hogan in the main event. The match drew a record-breaking crowd of over 93,000 fans at the Pontiac Silverdome. In a moment etched into wrestling history, Hogan body-slammed Andre and defeated him, ending his undefeated streak. The match solidified Andre's status as a legend and marked the passing of the torch to Hogan as wrestling's new megastar.

Despite his success, Andre faced significant challenges due to his size. He suffered from chronic pain, limited mobility, and health complications related to acromegaly. Traveling was particularly difficult, as he struggled to fit into cars, planes, and hotel accommodations. Yet, Andre rarely complained, often using humor to cope with his difficulties.

Outside the ring, Andre was known for his gentle nature and love of life. He was an avid card player and enjoyed spending time with friends, often regaling them with stories from his travels. His role as Fezzik in the 1987 film The Princess Bride showcased his charm and acting talent, earning him a new legion of fans.

Lesser-known facts about Andre include his legendary drinking capacity—he was said to have consumed over 100 beers in one sitting—and his generous spirit. He often paid for meals and drinks for entire groups, believing his success should be shared with those around him.

As his health declined, Andre wrestled less frequently, focusing on appearances and special matches. He retired from full-time competition in the early 1990s, but his impact on wrestling endured. On January 27, 1993, Andre passed away in his sleep from congestive heart failure while visiting France. He was 46 years old.

Andre's legacy lives on in the hearts of fans and wrestlers alike. He was the inaugural inductee into the WWE Hall of Fame in 1993, a fitting tribute to a man whose contributions to wrestling are immeasurable. His life story serves as a reminder of the power of resilience, kindness, and embracing one's uniqueness.

Andre the Giant's journey from a small French village to global stardom is a tale of extraordinary proportions. His larger-than-life presence, both in and out of the ring, continues to inspire generations, ensuring that the legend of Andre the Giant will never fade.

38. Goldberg: The Icon of Wrestling Power

Goldberg, born William Scott Goldberg on December 27, 1966, in Tulsa, Oklahoma, is one of the most dominant figures in the history of professional wrestling. Known for his explosive power, iconic winning streak, and no-nonsense persona, Goldberg became a household name in the wrestling world and a symbol of invincibility during his storied career.

William was the youngest of four children in a close-knit Jewish family. His father, Jed, was a doctor, and his mother, Ethel, was a concert violinist. Growing up in Tulsa, Goldberg was a multi-talented athlete who excelled in football. He attended Tulsa Edison High School, where his strength and speed set him apart on the football field. His passion for sports was evident, and his family supported his ambitions.

After high school, Goldberg attended the University of Georgia on a football scholarship, playing as a defensive tackle. His exceptional performance on the college football team earned him a spot in the NFL. In 1990, Goldberg was drafted by the Los Angeles Rams, and he later played for the Atlanta Falcons. However, his football career was cut short due to a severe abdominal injury. While this setback ended his NFL dreams, it opened the door to a new path that would change his life.

Goldberg's transition to professional wrestling began in the mid-1990s. Inspired by a chance meeting with wrestling legend Lex Luger, Goldberg decided to try his hand at wrestling. He trained under WCW (World Championship Wrestling) stars and quickly displayed an aptitude for the sport. His imposing physique, combined with his athletic background, made him an ideal candidate for the intense world of wrestling.

In 1997, Goldberg made his wrestling debut with WCW. From the moment he entered the ring, his raw power and intensity captivated audiences. WCW management wisely built him up as an unstoppable force, leading to his unprecedented winning streak. Goldberg's matches were often short and brutal, ending with his devastating finishing moves, the Spear and the Jackhammer.

Goldberg's undefeated streak became the stuff of legend, officially reaching 173-0 before being broken by Kevin Nash at Starrcade 1998. During his streak, Goldberg captured the WCW United States Heavyweight Championship and later the WCW World Heavyweight Championship, defeating Hulk Hogan in front of a massive crowd in Atlanta. The victory cemented his status as a wrestling megastar.

Despite his immense popularity, Goldberg faced challenges in WCW. Creative differences and the eventual decline of the company led to frustrations. After WCW was acquired by WWE in 2001, Goldberg took a hiatus from wrestling. He returned to the ring in 2003 with WWE, engaging in high-profile rivalries with The Rock, Triple H, and Brock Lesnar. His match against Lesnar at WrestleMania XX was memorable, though it marked the end of his first WWE stint.

After retiring from wrestling, Goldberg explored other ventures. He appeared in movies, including The Longest Yard and Santa's Slay, and became a commentator for MMA. Goldberg also dedicated time to philanthropy, advocating for animal welfare and supporting military veterans. His love for classic cars became a prominent part of his life, with his extensive car collection reflecting his passion for speed and style.

Goldberg made a triumphant return to WWE in 2016, reigniting his feud with Brock Lesnar. Their matches showcased Goldberg's enduring appeal and his ability to deliver thrilling performances. In 2018, Goldberg was inducted into the WWE Hall of Fame, a testament to his impact on the wrestling industry.

Lesser-known facts about Goldberg include his status as one of the few Jewish world champions in wrestling and his lifelong commitment to fitness. His ability to connect with fans, despite his limited mic work, highlighted the power of his physical presence and charisma.

As of now, Goldberg continues to make occasional appearances in WWE, proving that his legacy remains strong. His story is one of resilience, reinvention, and the pursuit of greatness, inspiring countless fans to push through challenges and embrace their strengths.

Goldberg's rise from a small-town athlete to a global wrestling icon is a testament to the power of perseverance and determination. His streak, his signature moves, and his no-nonsense attitude have secured his place in wrestling history, ensuring that the name Goldberg will forever echo in the annals of professional wrestling.

39. AJ Lee: The Unstoppable Underdog

AJ Lee, born April Jeanette Mendez on March 19, 1987, in Union City, New Jersey, rose from humble beginnings to become one of the most influential figures in women's wrestling. Known for her quick wit, high-energy performances, and captivating personality, AJ Lee redefined the role of women in WWE, leaving an indelible mark on the wrestling industry.

April grew up in a working-class Puerto Rican family, facing financial struggles that shaped her determination and resilience. Her parents, Robert and Janet Mendez, worked tirelessly to provide for their children, instilling in them the importance of hard work and perseverance. As a child, April found solace in wrestling, idolizing stars like Lita and Trish Stratus. She dreamed of one day stepping into the ring herself, even as she faced the harsh realities of her circumstances.

April attended Memorial High School in West New York, New Jersey, excelling academically while immersing herself in the world of wrestling. She later enrolled at New York University's Tisch School of the Arts, studying film and television production, but left due to financial constraints. Determined to pursue her wrestling dream, she began training at a local wrestling school in 2007.

AJ made her professional wrestling debut in 2008 on the independent circuit, performing under the ring name Miss April. Her tenacity and natural charisma quickly caught the attention of promoters, and in 2009, she signed a developmental contract with WWE. Assigned to Florida Championship Wrestling (FCW), WWE's developmental territory, AJ honed her skills and developed her "girl next door" persona.

AJ Lee's WWE main roster debut came in 2011 as part of the women's division. Initially portrayed as a sweet and bubbly underdog, AJ's career took a dramatic turn when she became embroiled in complex storylines involving high-profile wrestlers like Daniel Bryan, CM Punk, and Kane. Her sharp acting skills and unique character work made her stand out, earning her the nickname "The Crazy Chick."

AJ's in-ring abilities were equally impressive. Despite her small stature, she brought intensity and technical skill to her matches, proving that she could hold her own against larger opponents. Her signature moves, including the Black Widow submission hold, became fan favorites, showcasing her agility and creativity.

In 2013, AJ captured her first WWE Divas Championship, defeating Kaitlyn at Payback. Her victory marked the beginning of a record-breaking 295-day reign, during which she defended the title against numerous challengers. AJ's reign was a turning point for women's wrestling, as she emphasized athleticism and storytelling over superficiality.

AJ was a vocal advocate for women's wrestling, famously delivering a scathing "Pipe Bombshell" promo in 2014, calling out WWE's treatment of the women's division and demanding better opportunities for female wrestlers. Her words resonated with fans and paved the way for the Women's Revolution, which transformed the division into a showcase of athleticism and skill.

Despite her success, AJ faced challenges in her career. Her outspoken nature and association with her husband, CM Punk, often put her at odds with WWE management. Additionally, she dealt with personal struggles, including bipolar disorder, which she openly discussed to inspire others facing similar challenges.

AJ retired from in-ring competition in 2015, citing physical and personal reasons. Post-retirement, she became a bestselling author with her memoir Crazy Is My Superpower, detailing her journey and advocating for mental health awareness. AJ's work outside wrestling has included acting, writing, and advocating for animal welfare and anti-bullying initiatives.

Lesser-known facts about AJ include her love for comic books and video games, which she often incorporated into her wrestling persona. She was also a devoted fan of cosplay, frequently paying homage to her favorite characters in her outfits.

AJ Lee's legacy is one of empowerment and innovation. She was a trailblazer who refused to conform, challenging the status quo and inspiring a generation of wrestlers and fans. Her journey from a struggling teenager in New Jersey to a WWE icon is a testament to the power of resilience, authenticity, and believing in oneself.

Though retired, AJ's impact on wrestling endures. She remains a role model for aspiring wrestlers and a symbol of what can be achieved with determination and courage. AJ Lee's story is a reminder that being different is a strength, and sometimes, the smallest person in the ring can have the biggest voice.

40. Trish Stratus: The Queen of Women's Wrestling

Trish Stratus, born Patricia Anne Strategies on December 18, 1975, in Toronto, Ontario, Canada, is a legendary figure in professional wrestling. Known for her beauty, athleticism, and charisma, Trish broke barriers in the WWE and set a new standard for women in wrestling. Her journey from fitness model to seven-time WWE Women's Champion is a story of dedication, resilience, and passion.

Trish grew up in a supportive and loving family in Toronto, the eldest of three sisters. Her parents, John, and Alice Stratigeas, emphasized education and hard work. As a child, Trish was active in sports, excelling in soccer and field hockey. She attended York University, where she studied biology and kinesiology with plans to pursue a career in medicine. However, a faculty strike at the university disrupted her studies and led her to explore other opportunities.

While working as a receptionist at a gym, Trish was discovered by a fitness magazine publisher. Her natural beauty and fit physique catapulted her into the world of fitness modeling, where she became one of Canada's top fitness icons. Her magazine covers caught the attention of WWE executives, who saw her potential as a star in the wrestling world.

In 2000, Trish debuted in WWE as a manager, aligning herself with the tag team T&A (Test and Albert). While her initial role was primarily as eye candy, Trish was determined to prove she was more than just a pretty face. She began training rigorously in wrestling, working with experienced trainers to hone her skills. Her dedication paid off as she transitioned into an in-ring competitor.

Trish's first major match came at WrestleMania X-Seven in 2001, where she played a pivotal role in a storyline involving Vince McMahon and his family. While the match showcased her growing confidence, it was her subsequent matches that truly highlighted her improvement as a wrestler.

Over the years, Trish engaged in memorable rivalries with stars like Lita, Mickie James, and Victoria. Her feud with Lita is widely regarded as one of the greatest rivalries in women's wrestling history. Their main-event match on Monday Night Raw in 2004 was groundbreaking, as it was one of the first times women headlined WWE's flagship program.

Trish's accolades in WWE are unparalleled. She won the WWE Women's Championship seven times, a record during her era, and was named WWE's Diva of the Decade in 2003. Her in-ring style combined technical prowess, athleticism, and a flair for storytelling, making her a fan favorite and a role model for aspiring wrestlers.

Despite her success, Trish faced challenges throughout her career. Early on, she had to overcome stereotypes and prove that women could be both strong athletes and compelling entertainers. Injuries, including a serious back issue in 2005, tested her resilience, but Trish always returned stronger.

In 2006, Trish announced her retirement from full-time competition, choosing to step away at the peak of her career. Her final match at

LEGENDS OF THE WRESTLING RING

Unforgiven in her hometown of Toronto was a fairytale ending, as she defeated Lita to win her seventh Women's Championship. The emotional farewell was a testament to the love and respect she had earned from fans and peers.

Post-retirement, Trish focused on her personal life and business ventures. She married her high school sweetheart, Ron Fisico, in 2006, and the couple welcomed two children. Trish also launched a successful yoga studio, Stratusphere, combining her love for fitness and wellness.

Lesser-known facts about Trish include her philanthropic work. She is a passionate advocate for children's health and education, frequently supporting charitable initiatives. Trish is also an accomplished actress, appearing in films and television shows, showcasing her versatility beyond wrestling.

In 2013, Trish was inducted into the WWE Hall of Fame, solidifying her legacy as one of the greatest women in wrestling history. She returned to WWE for special appearances, including matches at WrestleMania and Evolution, WWE's first all-women's pay-per-view.

Trish Stratus's story is one of transformation and triumph. From a fitness model to a wrestling icon, she shattered stereotypes and paved the way for future generations of women in wrestling. Her legacy as a trailblazer and role model continues to inspire, proving that with determination and passion, anything is possible.

Trish remains active in various ventures, balancing her roles as a mother, entrepreneur, and wrestling legend. Her journey is a celebration of breaking barriers, embracing challenges, and striving for excellence. Trish Stratus is more than a champion—she is a symbol of empowerment and strength.

41. Lita: The Fearless Trailblazer

Lita, born Amy Christine Dumas on April 14, 1975, in Fort Lauderdale, Florida, is one of the most iconic and influential women in the history of professional wrestling. Known for her high-flying moves, punk-rock style, and fearless attitude, Lita shattered stereotypes and redefined the role of women in wrestling.

Amy's childhood was marked by a sense of independence and curiosity. Raised by a single mother, she moved frequently, adapting to new environments and finding solace in music and sports. She excelled in swimming and soccer during her high school years and developed a love for alternative music, which would later influence her unique persona in WWE.

After graduating from high school, Amy attended Georgia State University, studying education. However, her restless spirit led her to drop out and pursue a more adventurous path. She discovered wrestling while watching a match featuring Rey Mysterio, whose high-flying style captivated her. Inspired by his athleticism, Amy decided to pursue a career in professional wrestling, despite having no formal background in the sport.

LEGENDS OF THE WRESTLING RING

In the late 1990s, Amy trained under wrestler Dory Funk Jr. at his wrestling school, The Funkin' Conservatory, where she honed her skills and developed a daring in-ring style. She made her wrestling debut in Mexico, wrestling under the name "Angelica." Her time in Mexico exposed her to the lucha libre style, characterized by acrobatics and aerial maneuvers, which became a hallmark of her wrestling career.

Amy's big break came in 1999 when she signed with Extreme Championship Wrestling (ECW). Wrestling under the name Miss Congeniality, she showcased her potential but yearned for a larger platform. In 2000, she joined the World Wrestling Federation (WWF, now WWE), debuting as Lita alongside wrestler Essa Rios. Her fiery red hair, tattooed arms, and fearless moves quickly made her a fan favorite.

Lita's career reached new heights when she joined forces with The Hardy Boyz (Matt and Jeff Hardy), forming Team Xtreme. Together, they became one of the most popular acts in WWE, thrilling audiences with their high-risk moves and daredevil stunts. Lita's fearless dives and moonsaults set her apart from other female wrestlers, earning her the respect of fans and peers alike.

In 2001, Lita won her first WWE Women's Championship by defeating Stephanie McMahon on Raw. Her victory was a landmark moment, as she became a symbol of strength and empowerment for women in wrestling. Lita's rivalry with Trish Stratus, which spanned several years, is widely regarded as one of the greatest feuds in WWE history. Their matches, including a groundbreaking main event on Raw in 2004, showcased their athleticism and storytelling ability.

Despite her success, Lita faced significant challenges. Injuries, including a severe neck injury in 2002, threatened to end her career. She underwent surgery and extensive rehabilitation, demonstrating incredible resilience by returning to the ring stronger than ever. Lita also faced personal struggles, including public scrutiny over her relationships with wrestlers Matt Hardy and Edge, which were incorporated into controversial WWE storylines.

Lita retired from full-time competition in 2006 after losing her Women's Championship to Mickie James at Survivor Series. Her retirement marked the end of an era but did not diminish her influence on wrestling. She pursued other interests, including music, hosting a radio show, and fronting her punk band, The Luchagors.

Lesser-known facts about Lita include her love for animal rescue and her work as an advocate for women's rights. She has often spoken about the importance of self-expression and breaking boundaries, values that defined her career.

In 2014, Lita was inducted into the WWE Hall of Fame, cementing her legacy as one of the all-time greats. She continues to make occasional appearances in WWE, delighting fans with her charisma and timeless moves.

Lita's story is one of courage, innovation, and resilience. She inspired a generation of wrestlers to embrace their individuality and push the limits of what women can achieve in the ring. Lita's fearless spirit and trailblazing career ensure that her legacy will endure for generations to come.

42. Becky Lynch: Irish Lass Kicker 'The Man'

Becky Lynch, born Rebecca Quin on January 30, 1987, in Limerick, Ireland, is one of WWE's most celebrated and influential wrestlers. Known for her fiery personality, exceptional storytelling, and the moniker "The Man," Becky Lynch has transformed women's wrestling and inspired millions worldwide.

Rebecca grew up in Dublin, where she was raised alongside her older brother by hardworking parents. Her childhood was marked by an adventurous spirit and a love for sports, particularly swimming, basketball, and horse riding. However, her life took a challenging turn when her parents separated during her teenage years, prompting her to channel her energy into pursuits that would later shape her career.

Rebecca initially planned to become a physical education teacher and enrolled at the Dublin Institute of Technology. She studied acting and performed in local plays, showcasing a flair for the dramatic. However, her life took a different trajectory when her brother introduced her to professional wrestling. Instantly captivated, Rebecca saw wrestling as an art form combining athleticism, drama, and storytelling.

In 2002, at the age of 15, Rebecca began training at a wrestling school in Dublin run by Fergal Devitt (later known as Finn Bálor). Despite being one of the few women in the male-dominated world of wrestling, she trained tirelessly to prove herself. Her debut came later that year under the ring name Rebecca Knox, and her natural charisma and athletic ability quickly gained attention.

Rebecca wrestled across Europe and North America, competing in promotions such as NWA, Shimmer, and Japan's highly regarded wrestling circuits. Her high-flying moves and technical prowess made her a standout, but her rising career faced a significant setback in 2006 when she suffered a severe head injury during a match. The injury forced her to take a six-year hiatus from wrestling, during which she worked as an actress, stuntwoman, and flight attendant.

In 2013, Rebecca returned to wrestling and signed with WWE, reporting to its developmental territory, NXT. Rebranded as Becky Lynch, she initially struggled to find her footing. However, her perseverance and ability to adapt eventually paid off. By 2015, Becky was called up to WWE's main roster as part of the Women's Revolution, a movement aimed at showcasing women's wrestling as equal to men's.

Becky's rise to stardom was gradual but groundbreaking. Her turning point came in 2018 when she adopted the persona of "The Man," a confident and defiant character inspired by her desire to be recognized as the best wrestler, regardless of gender. The transformation resonated with fans, propelling her to superstardom. Her feud with Charlotte Flair and her iconic victory in the first women's WrestleMania main event in 2019, where she defeated Flair and Ronda Rousey to become Becky Two Belts, cemented her legacy.

Becky's achievements include holding the Raw Women's Championship for a record-setting 398 days, multiple Women's

Championships across WWE's brands, and headlining numerous pay-per-views. Her charisma, mic skills, and connection with the audience made her a trailblazer in women's wrestling.

Despite her success, Becky faced challenges throughout her career. Early struggles in WWE, injuries, and the pressure of representing a revolution tested her resolve. However, her determination to push boundaries and advocate for equal opportunities kept her moving forward.

Off-screen, Becky is known for her humility and wit. She married fellow WWE superstar Seth Rollins in 2021, and the couple welcomed their daughter, Roux, later that year. Becky's return to WWE after giving birth showcased her resilience and dedication to her craft.

Lesser-known facts about Becky include her background in martial arts, her love for video games, and her talent for cutting promos, which she attributes to her acting training. She is also an advocate for mental health awareness, often sharing her journey to inspire others.

Becky Lynch's legacy is one of empowerment and excellence. She has not only elevated women's wrestling but has also challenged traditional narratives in sports entertainment. Her story reminds fans that with hard work, authenticity, and passion, it's possible to overcome any obstacle and become "The Man."

43. Charlotte Flair: The Queen of the Ring

Charlotte Flair, born Ashley Elizabeth Fliehr on April 5, 1986, in Charlotte, North Carolina, is one of the most accomplished and charismatic wrestlers in WWE history. Known as "The Queen," Charlotte has carved out her own legacy, stepping out from the shadow of her legendary father, Ric Flair, and becoming a trailblazer for women in wrestling.

Ashley grew up in a family steeped in wrestling history. Her father, Ric Flair, was one of the most celebrated wrestlers of all time, known as "The Nature Boy." Despite her famous lineage, Ashley's childhood was relatively grounded, filled with athletic pursuits and a close bond with her siblings. She excelled in sports, particularly volleyball, and attended Providence High School, where she was a standout athlete.

After high school, Ashley pursued a degree in public relations at North Carolina State University while continuing her athletic career. She initially had no intentions of following in her father's footsteps, focusing instead on academics and sports. However, a personal tragedy changed the course of her life. Her younger brother, Reid Flair, who had dreams of wrestling stardom, passed away in 2013. Inspired to honor his memory, Ashley decided to step into the wrestling world.

Ashley began training at WWE's Performance Center, where her athleticism and determination set her apart. Adopting the ring name Charlotte, she made her in-ring debut in NXT, WWE's developmental brand, in 2013. Her first match showcased her natural talent and flair for storytelling, earning her praise from fans and critics alike.

Charlotte's rise in NXT was meteoric. She captured the NXT Women's Championship in 2014, defeating Natalya in a match that is still celebrated as a turning point for women's wrestling. Her technical skill, combined with her commanding presence, made her a star in the making.

In 2015, Charlotte debuted on WWE's main roster as part of the Women's Revolution, alongside Becky Lynch and Sasha Banks. This movement aimed to redefine women's wrestling, moving away from gimmicks and focusing on athletic competition. Charlotte quickly established herself as a dominant force, capturing the Divas Championship and later the Raw Women's Championship.

Charlotte's career has been defined by her numerous accomplishments and rivalries. She has won the WWE Women's Championship multiple times, holding the title in various brands, including Raw, SmackDown, and NXT. Her battles with Sasha Banks, Becky Lynch, and Bayley have produced some of the most memorable matches in WWE history.

One of Charlotte's most iconic moments came at WrestleMania 32, where she defeated Sasha Banks and Becky Lynch to become the inaugural WWE Women's Champion, retiring the Divas Championship in the process. This victory marked a new era for women's wrestling, with Charlotte at the forefront.

Despite her success, Charlotte has faced significant challenges. Being the daughter of Ric Flair brought immense pressure and comparisons, but she worked tirelessly to establish her own identity. Injuries and personal setbacks, including the loss of her brother, tested her resilience. Through it all, Charlotte's dedication to her craft and her ability to connect with fans kept her at the top of her game.

Outside the ring, Charlotte is known for her philanthropy and advocacy work. She is a strong supporter of mental health awareness and often speaks about the importance of self-confidence and perseverance. Her autobiography, Second Nature, co-written with her father, provides an intimate look at her journey and the lessons she has learned.

Lesser-known facts about Charlotte include her love for fitness and fashion, which she often incorporates into her wrestling persona. She is also a passionate advocate for women's rights, using her platform to inspire young girls to pursue their dreams fearlessly.

Charlotte Flair's story is one of determination, resilience, and excellence. She has not only elevated women's wrestling but has also become a symbol of empowerment and strength. Her ability to overcome adversity and thrive in the face of challenges is a testament to her character and dedication.

As "The Queen," Charlotte continues to reign supreme in WWE, inspiring fans and setting new standards for greatness. Her journey is a reminder that legacy is not just inherited—it is earned through hard work, passion, and an unyielding commitment to being the best.

44. Sasha Banks: The Boss of WWE

Sasha Banks, born Mercedes Justine Kaestner-Varnado on January 26, 1992, in Fairfield, California, is one of the most celebrated and charismatic figures in professional wrestling. Known as "The Boss," Sasha redefined women's wrestling with her unmatched athleticism, groundbreaking achievements, and unapologetic confidence.

Mercedes grew up in a military family, frequently moving between states and cities. Her early years were shaped by her close bond with her family, particularly her younger brother, who has autism. Her mother, Judith, and her father, Reo, instilled in her the values of resilience and determination. From a young age, Mercedes found solace in professional wrestling, idolizing stars like Eddie Guerrero, who became her inspiration to pursue the sport.

Despite the challenges of frequent relocations, Mercedes excelled in school and developed a strong work ethic. She was homeschooled to better accommodate her brother's needs, showcasing her selflessness and maturity at a young age. Wrestling, however, remained her ultimate passion. Determined to make her dream a reality, she began training in wrestling at just 18 years old.

Mercedes made her wrestling debut in 2010 for Chaotic Wrestling, an independent promotion based in Massachusetts. Wrestling under the name Mercedes KV, she quickly gained attention for her natural charisma and in-ring abilities. Her first significant achievement came in 2011 when she won the Chaotic Wrestling Women's Championship, establishing herself as a rising star on the independent circuit.

In 2012, Mercedes signed with WWE, reporting to its developmental brand, NXT. Rebranded as Sasha Banks, she adopted the persona of "The Boss," a confident and stylish character inspired by her love for hip-hop and fashion. Sasha's unique blend of arrogance and determination resonated with fans, setting her apart from other wrestlers.

Sasha's career in NXT was marked by her evolution as a performer. Her rivalry with Bayley culminated in a historic match at NXT TakeOver: Respect in 2015, where they competed in the first-ever women's Iron Man match in WWE history. This match, widely regarded as one of the greatest in NXT history, solidified Sasha's status as a trailblazer in women's wrestling.

Sasha's transition to WWE's main roster in 2015 coincided with the Women's Revolution, a movement aimed at showcasing women as equal competitors to men. Sasha quickly became a fan favorite, capturing her first WWE Women's Championship in 2016 by defeating Charlotte Flair. Their rivalry became one of the defining storylines of the era, producing several classic matches, including the first women's Hell in a Cell match.

Throughout her career, Sasha has amassed numerous accolades, including multiple Women's Championships on Raw and SmackDown, and the WWE Women's Tag Team Championship alongside her close friend Bayley. Together, they formed "The Golden Role Models," a dynamic duo that dominated WWE's women's division.

LEGENDS OF THE WRESTLING RING

Despite her success, Sasha faced significant challenges. Injuries and the grueling WWE schedule took a toll on her physically and mentally. In 2019, she took a hiatus from WWE to prioritize her well-being, a decision that highlighted the importance of self-care in a demanding industry. Her return later that year was met with overwhelming support from fans.

Lesser-known facts about Sasha include her love for anime and her role as a pioneer for representation in wrestling. As one of the first African American women to headline WWE's biggest events, Sasha broke barriers and inspired countless fans worldwide. Her role as Koska Reeves in The Mandalorian further showcased her versatility and charisma beyond the wrestling ring.

Sasha's legacy in WWE is defined by her ability to elevate women's wrestling to new heights. Her fearless approach to storytelling and her commitment to delivering memorable performances have earned her the respect of peers and fans alike. She has been a vocal advocate for equality and representation, using her platform to inspire positive change.

As of now, Sasha Banks continues to redefine what it means to be a wrestler, balancing her passion for the sport with her growing presence in the entertainment industry. Her story is a testament to the power of perseverance, authenticity, and believing in oneself. Sasha Banks is not just "The Boss"—she is a symbol of empowerment and excellence in every arena she steps into.

45. Bayley: The Hugger Who Transformed WWE

Bayley, born Pamela Rose Martinez on June 15, 1989, in Newark, California, is one of WWE's most endearing and accomplished wrestlers. Known for her unique transition from the cheerful "Hugger" to a devious role model, Bayley has etched her name into wrestling history with her versatility, talent, and charisma.

Pamela grew up in a tight-knit Mexican-American family in San Jose, California. As a child, she was a massive wrestling fan, idolizing stars like The Hardy Boyz, Lita, and Eddie Guerrero. She often attended wrestling events with her father, sparking a dream of one day stepping into the ring herself. Pamela was also an athlete, excelling in basketball and cross-country during high school, but wrestling remained her true passion.

After graduating from Independence High School, Pamela began training to become a wrestler at the age of 18. She enrolled at Big Time Wrestling's training school in Fremont, California, under the guidance

LEGENDS OF THE WRESTLING RING

of Jason Styles. Balancing her training with part-time jobs, she spent hours perfecting her craft, determined to make her dream a reality.

Bayley made her professional wrestling debut in 2008, wrestling under her real name for Big Time Wrestling. Her bubbly personality and hard-hitting style quickly made her a fan favorite on the independent circuit. Over the next few years, she competed in various promotions, honing her skills and building her reputation.

In 2012, Pamela signed with WWE and was assigned to NXT, WWE's developmental brand. Adopting the ring name Bayley, she debuted as a wide-eyed, enthusiastic underdog who loved hugs and inspiring fans. Though initially underestimated, Bayley's hard work and charisma won over the NXT audience.

Bayley's turning point in NXT came in 2015 during her rivalry with Sasha Banks. Their match at NXT TakeOver: Brooklyn, where Bayley defeated Sasha to win the NXT Women's Championship, is widely regarded as one of the best women's wrestling matches of all time. The emotional bout showcased Bayley's storytelling ability and earned her widespread acclaim.

Bayley's success in NXT paved the way for her main roster debut in 2016. She quickly became a key figure in WWE's Women's Revolution, which emphasized athleticism and equality in women's wrestling. Bayley's infectious energy and connection with fans made her a standout on Raw and SmackDown.

In 2017, Bayley captured the Raw Women's Championship, defeating Charlotte Flair at Fastlane. Her victory was a milestone, as she became the first woman to win the Raw, SmackDown, and NXT Women's Championships. Bayley's journey resonated with fans, particularly young girls, who saw her as a role model.

However, Bayley's career took an unexpected turn in 2019 when she reinvented herself as a villain. She cut her signature ponytail, destroyed her "Bayley Buddies," and adopted a more cynical persona. This transformation shocked fans but revitalized her career, allowing her to explore new depths as a performer. As a villain, Bayley captured the SmackDown Women's Championship and became one of the most dominant champions in WWE history.

Bayley's accolades include multiple Women's Championships, the WWE Women's Tag Team Championship (with Sasha Banks), and historic moments like competing in the first-ever women's WarGames match. Her versatility and consistency have earned her praise as one of the best wrestlers of her generation.

Despite her success, Bayley faced challenges, including injuries and the pressure of constantly evolving her character. Her ability to overcome adversity and adapt to new roles has been a testament to her resilience and creativity.

Lesser-known facts about Bayley include her love for video games, her dedication to inspiring young fans, and her role as a mentor to up-and-coming wrestlers. Off-screen, Pamela is known for her humility and strong work ethic, qualities that have endeared her to fans and peers alike.

Bayley's story is one of determination, reinvention, and staying true to oneself. From her days as an underdog in NXT to becoming a trailblazer in WWE, Bayley has proven that authenticity and hard work can lead to greatness. Her legacy as a wrestler who broke barriers and captured hearts will endure for years to come.

46. The Miz: From Reality Star to WWE Icon

Michael Gregory Mizanin, better known as The Miz, was born on October 8, 1980, in Parma, Ohio. From humble beginnings, he rose to fame as one of WWE's most recognizable and polarizing figures, combining charisma, resilience, and undeniable talent to carve out a unique legacy in professional wrestling.

Michael grew up in a middle-class family, the son of Barbara and George Mizanin. His parents divorced when he was young, but both remained a significant influence in his life. Michael excelled at sports, playing basketball and running cross-country at Normandy High School. He was also involved in student government, serving as class president.

After high school, Michael attended Miami University in Ohio, where he studied business. However, he felt unfulfilled and yearned for something more dynamic. His life took an unexpected turn when he auditioned for MTV's reality show The Real World: Back to New York in 2001. Selected for the show, Michael quickly became known for his brash and outspoken personality. During his time on The Real World and its spin-off, The Challenge, he introduced his alter ego, "The Miz," a character he developed to showcase his larger-than-life persona.

Inspired by his love of wrestling, Michael decided to pursue a career in the sport. Despite skepticism from fans and peers due to his reality TV background, he joined Ultimate Pro Wrestling (UPW) in 2003, training rigorously to prove himself. In 2004, he competed in WWE's reality competition Tough Enough, finishing as the runner-up but earning a developmental contract with the company.

The Miz made his WWE debut in 2006, initially hosting segments and competing in mid-card matches. He faced criticism from fans and fellow wrestlers, many of whom doubted his abilities and questioned his place in the industry. Undeterred, The Miz worked tirelessly to improve his in-ring skills and develop his character, using his natural charisma and gift for mic work to stand out.

The Miz's breakthrough came in 2010 when he won the Money in the Bank contract, which he successfully cashed in to defeat Randy Orton for the WWE Championship. His reign as champion was capped off with a main-event victory at WrestleMania XXVII, where he defeated John Cena with an assist from The Rock. This triumph silenced critics and solidified The Miz as a top-tier talent.

Throughout his career, The Miz has achieved numerous accolades, including multiple Intercontinental Championships, Tag Team Championships, and a second WWE Championship reign in 2021. He is one of WWE's most decorated stars, known for his versatility and ability to elevate storylines. His partnerships with wrestlers like John Morrison and Maryse, his real-life wife, have added layers to his persona and created memorable moments.

The Miz's career has been marked by resilience and reinvention. He transitioned from a hated villain to a respected veteran, earning the admiration of fans and peers. His work ethic and dedication to his craft have made him a role model for aspiring wrestlers, showing that perseverance and self-belief can overcome doubt.

Outside the ring, The Miz has showcased his talents as a host and actor. He starred in The Marine film series and hosted reality shows like WWE Tough Enough and Cannonball. Alongside Maryse, he stars in the hit reality show Miz & Mrs., offering fans a glimpse into their personal lives.

Lesser-known facts about The Miz include his passion for Cleveland sports teams and his philanthropy work, particularly with the Make-A-Wish Foundation. Despite his flashy persona, Michael is grounded and values his role as a father to his two daughters, Monroe and Madison.

The Miz's story is one of persistence and evolution. From reality TV underdog to WWE mainstay, he defied expectations and became a symbol of resilience. His ability to adapt and entertain has made him a cornerstone of WWE, ensuring his legacy will endure for years to come.

47. Kevin Owens: The Relentless Prizefighter

Kevin Owens, born Kevin Steen on May 7, 1984, in Saint-Jean-sur-Richelieu, Quebec, Canada, is a professional wrestler celebrated for his grit, determination, and ability to connect with audiences. Known for his unorthodox style and relentless attitude, Owens has become a mainstay in WWE, earning accolades and respect as a versatile performer.

Kevin grew up in a French-speaking household, the son of parents Terry and Suzanne Steen. His family later moved to Marieville, Quebec, where Kevin developed a love for sports, particularly hockey and wrestling. As a child, Kevin idolized wrestlers like Steve Austin, The Rock, and Owen Hart, finding inspiration in their charisma and physicality.

At 14, Kevin decided to pursue wrestling after watching a match between Shawn Michaels and Diesel at WrestleMania XI. Encouraged by his supportive parents, he began training under Serge Jodoin, a former wrestler based in Quebec. Kevin's dedication was evident from the start; despite being an unconventional athlete, he displayed remarkable agility, strength, and an innate understanding of wrestling psychology.

Kevin made his professional wrestling debut in 2000 at the age of 16, performing under his real name in local Quebec promotions. Over the next decade, he built a reputation as one of the most talented independent wrestlers in North America. Adopting the ring name Kevin Steen, he competed in promotions such as Pro Wrestling Guerrilla (PWG) and Ring of Honor (ROH), where he became a fan favorite for his fearless style and sharp mic skills.

In ROH, Kevin formed a successful tag team with El Generico (now known as Sami Zayn), capturing the ROH World Tag Team Championship. Their partnership eventually turned into one of wrestling's most storied rivalries, producing intense matches that showcased Kevin's ability to tell compelling stories in the ring. He also held the ROH World Championship, further solidifying his status as a top-tier talent.

Kevin's big break came in 2014 when he signed with WWE and joined NXT, the company's developmental brand. Rebranded as Kevin Owens, he made an immediate impact, debuting in December of that year and capturing the NXT Championship just two months later by defeating Sami Zayn. His dominant performance and intense rivalry with Zayn introduced him to a global audience.

In 2015, Kevin made his main roster debut on Monday Night Raw, where he shocked the world by defeating John Cena in his first match. This victory catapulted Kevin into the spotlight, and he quickly became one of WWE's most compelling characters. Known as "The Prizefighter," Kevin's persona emphasized his focus on winning championships and providing for his family.

Over the years, Kevin has won multiple titles in WWE, including the Universal Championship, Intercontinental Championship, and United States Championship. His feuds with top stars like Seth

Rollins, Roman Reigns, and Chris Jericho have produced some of WWE's most memorable moments. His friendship-turned-rivalry with Jericho, culminating in the "Festival of Friendship" storyline, remains one of the most critically acclaimed angles in WWE history.

Despite his success, Kevin's journey has not been without challenges. His unconventional physique and straightforward demeanor initially led some to doubt his potential as a main event star. However, Kevin silenced critics through his consistent performances, proving that passion and talent matter more than appearances. He also dealt with injuries, including a knee surgery in 2018, which temporarily sidelined him but didn't diminish his drive.

Kevin is known for his authenticity, both in and out of the ring. A devoted family man, he often credits his wife, Karina, and their two children, Owen and Élodie, as his greatest sources of motivation. His connection to his family is evident in his ring name, which he chose to honor his son.

Lesser-known facts about Kevin include his proficiency in French, his love for music, and his passion for promoting inclusivity in wrestling. He often uses his platform to advocate for respect and diversity, resonating with fans around the world.

Kevin Owens' legacy is one of resilience and reinvention. From his humble beginnings in Quebec to becoming a global wrestling icon, he has consistently defied expectations and delivered unforgettable moments. His ability to connect with audiences, coupled with his unrelenting determination, ensures that Kevin Owens' story will continue to inspire for generations to come.

48. Shinsuke Nakamura: The King of Strong Style

Shinsuke Nakamura, born on February 24, 1980, in Mineyama, Kyoto Prefecture, Japan, is a professional wrestler renowned for his flamboyant personality, electrifying charisma, and mastery of the "Strong Style." With a career spanning multiple decades and continents, Nakamura is celebrated as one of the most influential wrestlers of his generation.

Nakamura grew up in a close-knit family in Kyoto. His parents, supportive of his aspirations, encouraged his active lifestyle. As a child, Shinsuke excelled in sports, particularly in martial arts and judo, where he developed the discipline and resilience that would later define his career. He attended Mineyama High School and later enrolled at Aoyama Gakuin University, where he pursued his passion for physical education.

While in university, Nakamura became enamored with professional wrestling, inspired by Japanese legends such as Antonio Inoki and Tatsumi Fujinami. Determined to pursue his dream, he joined the New

Japan Pro-Wrestling (NJPW) dojo in 2002. At 6'2" and with a lean but powerful build, Nakamura was a natural athlete who quickly adapted to the rigorous training regimen.

Shinsuke made his professional debut on August 29, 2002, against Tadao Yasuda. From the outset, his charisma and unorthodox style set him apart. He was soon dubbed the "Super Rookie" for his rapid ascent in NJPW. By 2003, Nakamura won his first IWGP Heavyweight Championship, becoming one of the youngest wrestlers to achieve this feat at just 23 years old.

Nakamura's in-ring style, known as "Strong Style," emphasized hard-hitting strikes and technical precision. He incorporated elements of MMA into his repertoire, reflecting his background in mixed martial arts, which included training and a handful of professional fights. His unique blend of martial arts and wrestling made him a formidable competitor and a fan favorite.

Throughout the 2000s, Nakamura established himself as a cornerstone of NJPW, capturing multiple IWGP Heavyweight Championships and headlining major events like Wrestle Kingdom. His rivalries with Hiroshi Tanahashi, Kazuchika Okada, and AJ Styles produced some of the most memorable matches in wrestling history. Nakamura also played a pivotal role in popularizing NJPW on a global scale, earning accolades for his technical prowess and captivating entrances.

One of Nakamura's defining characteristics was his showmanship. His theatrical entrances, often featuring elaborate costumes and dance-like movements, became a hallmark of his persona. Coupled with his signature "YeaOh!" chant and exaggerated mannerisms, Nakamura's charisma transcended language barriers, making him a global sensation. In 2016, Nakamura signed with WWE, debuting in NXT. His first match, against Sami Zayn at NXT TakeOver: Dallas, was hailed as an instant classic and showcased his ability to adapt his style to a new audience. Nakamura quickly became NXT Champion, cementing his status as a top-tier performer.

LEGENDS OF THE WRESTLING RING

Nakamura's main roster debut in WWE came in 2017 on SmackDown. He made an immediate impact, with his feud against AJ Styles culminating in a series of high-profile matches, including a WWE Championship bout at WrestleMania 34. Nakamura also captured the United States Championship and the Intercontinental Championship, further solidifying his legacy.

Despite his success, Nakamura faced challenges, including adapting to WWE's style and schedule. His decision to move to the United States with his family was driven by a desire for new opportunities and to broaden his appeal. Nakamura's ability to navigate these challenges highlighted his resilience and adaptability.

Lesser-known facts about Nakamura include his passion for surfing, his love for Michael Jackson (which influenced his entrance style), and his talent as an artist. He is also a published author, having written an autobiography detailing his journey and philosophy on wrestling.

Shinsuke Nakamura's legacy is one of innovation and artistry. As the "King of Strong Style," he redefined what it means to be a wrestler, blending athleticism, entertainment, and cultural flair. His impact extends beyond championships and accolades, inspiring a new generation of wrestlers to embrace their individuality and push the boundaries of the sport.

Even as his career continues, Nakamura remains a global icon whose influence resonates in every corner of the wrestling world. His story is a testament to the power of passion, creativity, and staying true to oneself.

49. Braun Strowman: The Monster Among Men

Braun Strowman, born Adam Joseph Scherr on September 6, 1983, in Sherrills Ford, North Carolina, is a professional wrestler known for his towering presence, raw power, and electrifying performances. Nicknamed "The Monster Among Men," Strowman became a force to be reckoned with in WWE, captivating fans with his unparalleled strength and larger-than-life persona.

Adam grew up in a small town in North Carolina, the son of Sara and Rick Scherr. His father, Rick, was a legendary softball player, which instilled a competitive spirit in Adam from an early age. Growing up, he was an athletic and adventurous child, excelling in sports like football, track and field, and wrestling during his high school years at Bandys High School.

After graduating in 2001, Adam pursued a semi-professional football career, playing for the Hickory Hornets. He later attended the NFL Scouting Combine in 2007 but did not secure a spot in the league.

LEGENDS OF THE WRESTLING RING

Despite this setback, Adam shifted his focus to strength sports, where his imposing 6'8" frame and raw power set him apart.

Adam began competing in strongman competitions, quickly making a name for himself in the sport. In 2011, he won the Arnold Amateur Strongman World Championship, which earned him a spot in professional-level competitions. His feats of strength, including pulling trucks and lifting massive weights, showcased his incredible physical abilities.

Adam's entry into professional wrestling came in 2013 when he signed with WWE. Rebranded as Braun Strowman, he began training at the WWE Performance Center. His wrestling career officially launched in 2014 when he appeared as a member of the Rosebuds entourage on Raw. However, it was his debut in 2015 as part of The Wyatt Family that introduced him to a global audience.

Braun's initial role as the muscle of The Wyatt Family highlighted his dominance and mysterious aura. Standing at nearly seven feet tall and weighing over 300 pounds, Braun quickly became a formidable presence in WWE. His first major match came at Night of Champions 2015, where he helped The Wyatt Family secure a victory against Roman Reigns, Dean Ambrose, and Chris Jericho.

Braun's solo career began in 2016 after The Wyatt Family disbanded. WWE showcased his monstrous persona by pitting him against local wrestlers in squash matches, building his reputation as an unstoppable force. His feuds with Roman Reigns, Brock Lesnar, and Kane solidified his status as a main-event star.

One of Braun's most iconic moments came in 2018 when he won the Greatest Royal Rumble in Saudi Arabia, eliminating 13 opponents and setting a record. He also captured the WWE Universal Championship in 2020 by defeating Goldberg at WrestleMania 36, a crowning achievement in his career.

Braun's strength and charisma made him a fan favorite, but his journey was not without challenges. Injuries, including knee and elbow issues, tested his resilience. Additionally, his unconventional rise from strongman to wrestler drew skepticism from purists. However, Braun silenced critics with his dedication and ability to deliver memorable performances.

Off-screen, Braun is known for his humor, humility, and love for outdoor activities like hunting and fishing. He has also been a vocal advocate for mental health awareness, often sharing his own struggles to inspire others.

Lesser-known facts about Braun include his passion for custom motorcycles and his nickname "Country Strong," reflecting his rural roots and immense strength. Despite his intimidating persona, he is known to be approachable and kind-hearted, earning respect from fans and colleagues alike.

Braun Strowman's story is one of transformation and triumph. From his beginnings in a small town to becoming a global wrestling icon, he embodies the values of hard work, perseverance, and staying true to oneself. As "The Monster Among Men," Braun Strowman has left an indelible mark on WWE and continues to inspire with his journey.

50. Ricky Steamboat: The Dragon's Legacy

Ricky Steamboat, born Richard Henry Blood on February 28, 1953, in West Point, New York, is one of the most celebrated professional wrestlers in history. Known as "The Dragon," Steamboat captivated audiences with his athleticism, charisma, and storytelling, becoming a symbol of excellence in wrestling during his illustrious career.

Richard grew up in a military family, with his father serving in the United States Army. His family frequently moved, which taught him adaptability and resilience from an early age. Eventually, they settled in Florida, where Richard attended high school. He excelled in sports, particularly wrestling, earning accolades at the state level. His natural talent and competitive spirit hinted at the greatness that awaited him.

After high school, Ricky pursued further education but remained deeply involved in sports. His passion for wrestling led him to train under the legendary Verne Gagne, who recognized his potential and guided him into the professional wrestling world. Steamboat made his debut in 1976 in the American Wrestling Association (AWA), wrestling under his real name. However, upon joining Championship

Wrestling from Florida, he adopted the ring name Ricky Steamboat, a nod to wrestler Sam Steamboat.

Ricky's career took off when he joined Jim Crockett Promotions, where he became a star in the National Wrestling Alliance (NWA). Known for his high-flying moves, technical prowess, and natural charisma, Steamboat quickly became a fan favorite. His rivalry with Ric Flair in the 1980s is widely regarded as one of the greatest in wrestling history. Their matches, including the trilogy in 1989, are celebrated for their storytelling, athleticism, and intensity.

Steamboat's ability to connect with audiences stemmed from his relatable persona. Unlike many larger-than-life characters of the era, Ricky portrayed himself as an honorable and hardworking competitor. His iconic feud with "Macho Man" Randy Savage culminated in their legendary match at WrestleMania III in 1987, which is still considered one of the greatest matches in WWE history. Steamboat's victory for the Intercontinental Championship cemented his status as a wrestling legend.

Throughout his career, Ricky captured numerous titles, including the NWA World Heavyweight Championship, the Intercontinental Championship, and several Tag Team Championships. He partnered with stars like Jay Youngblood and Dusty Rhodes, delivering memorable matches that showcased his versatility and teamwork.

Despite his success, Ricky faced challenges, including injuries that tested his resilience. A severe back injury in the early 1990s forced him to step away from the ring temporarily. However, his determination brought him back, and he continued to compete at a high level, even as the wrestling landscape evolved.

Lesser-known facts about Ricky include his love for martial arts, which influenced his "Dragon" persona. His dramatic entrances often featured him breathing fire, adding a theatrical element that thrilled fans. Outside the ring, Ricky is known for his humility and dedication to his family. He has a son, Richie Steamboat, who also pursued a wrestling career, carrying on his father's legacy.

Ricky's insights and values centered on professionalism and respect. He often emphasized the importance of storytelling and connecting with the audience, believing that wrestling was as much about emotion as it was about physicality. His clean-cut image and commitment to fair play made him a role model for fans and peers alike.

Steamboat retired from active competition in the mid-1990s but continued to contribute to wrestling as a trainer and mentor. He made occasional appearances in WWE, including a memorable return at WrestleMania 25 in 2009, where he reminded fans of his timeless talent.

Ricky Steamboat's legacy is one of integrity, excellence, and passion. As "The Dragon," he inspired generations of wrestlers and fans, proving that dedication and authenticity can create a lasting impact. His story remains a testament to the power of hard work, resilience, and staying true to oneself.

51. Dusty Rhodes: The American Dream

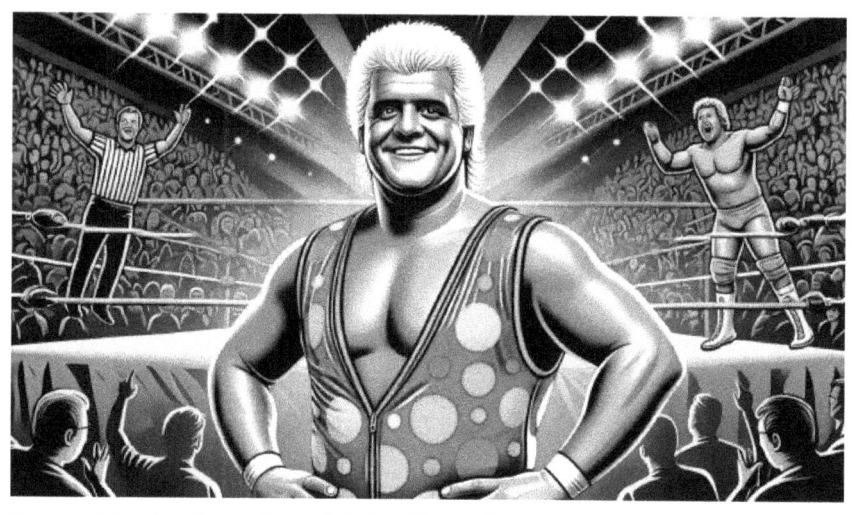

Dusty Rhodes, born Virgil Riley Runnels Jr. on October 11, 1945, in Austin, Texas, was one of the most beloved and influential professional wrestlers in history. Known as "The American Dream," Rhodes captivated audiences with his charisma, resilience, and ability to connect with fans from all walks of life. His story is one of determination, passion, and the pursuit of a dream.

Virgil grew up in a modest household in Austin. His father, Virgil Sr., worked as a plumber, while his mother, Elizabeth, managed the home. Dusty was raised with strong values of hard work and humility, which later became cornerstones of his wrestling persona. As a child, Dusty was an energetic and athletic boy, excelling in football and baseball during his school years.

After graduating from high school, Dusty attended West Texas State University (now West Texas A&M University), where he played football as a lineman. His natural athletic ability and larger-than-life personality made him a standout, but he yearned for something more than sports. Inspired by the wrestling legends he watched as a child, Dusty decided to pursue a career in professional wrestling.

LEGENDS OF THE WRESTLING RING

Dusty began his wrestling journey in 1968, debuting in the American Wrestling Association (AWA). Initially performing as a heel (villain), Dusty's quick wit and ability to engage with the audience set him apart. It wasn't long before he found his calling as a babyface (hero), portraying the working-class everyman who fought for the people.

Dusty's defining moment came when he adopted the moniker "The American Dream." This character resonated deeply with fans, as Dusty embodied the hopes and struggles of everyday people. With his Southern charm, iconic lisp, and emotional promos, Dusty could captivate audiences like few others. His ability to connect with fans was unmatched, earning him a loyal following.

Dusty's career reached new heights in the 1970s and 1980s while wrestling for promotions like the National Wrestling Alliance (NWA) and Jim Crockett Promotions. He became a three-time NWA World Heavyweight Champion, battling legends like Ric Flair, Harley Race, and Terry Funk. His feud with Flair, in particular, is remembered as one of wrestling's greatest rivalries, with Dusty often representing the underdog against Flair's flashy, arrogant persona.

One of Dusty's most famous matches was the "Hard Times" promo and subsequent feud with Ric Flair, culminating in a victory at Starrcade 1985. Dusty's ability to tell stories through his words and matches made him a legend in the industry. His signature move, the Bionic Elbow, became a fan favorite, symbolizing his larger-than-life persona.

Dusty also played a significant role behind the scenes as a booker and creative mind. His vision helped shape some of wrestling's most iconic events, including the creation of Starrcade and the WarGames match format. Dusty's creativity and understanding of wrestling psychology made him a driving force in the industry.

Despite his success, Dusty faced challenges throughout his career. Injuries, financial struggles, and changes in the wrestling landscape tested his resilience. However, Dusty's unwavering belief in his dreams and his ability to adapt kept him relevant for decades.

In the late 1980s and early 1990s, Dusty joined WWE, where he famously donned polka-dot attire as part of his character. While some viewed this as a step-down, Dusty embraced the gimmick with his trademark charisma, proving that his personality could shine through any situation.

Dusty retired from full-time wrestling in the 1990s but remained active as a mentor and creative figure. He joined WWE's developmental program, helping to train future stars, including his sons Dustin (Goldust) and Cody Rhodes. Dusty's influence extended to generations of wrestlers who credit him as a source of inspiration and guidance.

Lesser-known facts about Dusty include his love for music, particularly country, and his role as a motivational speaker. He often spoke about the importance of dreaming big and working hard, values that defined his life and career.

Dusty Rhodes passed away on June 11, 2015, in Orlando, Florida, at the age of 69. His death marked the end of an era, but his legacy lives on through his contributions to wrestling and the memories he created for fans worldwide.

Dusty's story is a testament to the power of perseverance and authenticity. As "The American Dream," he inspired millions to chase their dreams, proving that with heart and determination, anything is possible. His legacy as a wrestler, storyteller, and icon will forever be etched in the annals of wrestling history.

52. Bob Backlund: The Champion of Discipline

Bob Backlund, born Robert Louis Backlund on August 14, 1949, in Princeton, Minnesota, is one of professional wrestling's most respected and enduring figures. Known for his unmatched discipline, technical prowess, and humble demeanor, Backlund carved out a legacy as a pure athlete and a dedicated champion.

Bob grew up in a small farming town in Minnesota, where hard work and perseverance were instilled in him from a young age. His parents, Doris and Lou Backlund were hardworking and encouraged their children to pursue education and sports. Bob's athletic journey began in high school, where he excelled in football and amateur wrestling. His strong work ethic and natural talent made him a standout in both disciplines.

After high school, Bob attended Waldorf College in Iowa, where he played football and continued wrestling. He later transferred to North Dakota State University, where he became an NCAA Division II wrestling champion in 1971. His success in amateur wrestling fueled his desire to explore professional wrestling, a sport that combined athleticism with showmanship.

Bob began his professional wrestling career in 1973, debuting in the American Wrestling Association (AWA). His clean-cut image, combined with his technical wrestling skills, made him an instant favorite. Bob's first significant match was against seasoned wrestler Harley Race, where his performance earned him recognition as a rising star.

In 1977, Bob joined the World Wide Wrestling Federation (WWWF), now known as WWE. Under the guidance of Vince McMahon Sr., he was groomed to become the company's next major star. Bob's wholesome image and incredible stamina resonated with fans, and he quickly ascended the ranks. On February 20, 1978, Backlund defeated Superstar Billy Graham to win the WWF World Heavyweight Championship. This victory marked the beginning of one of the longest and most successful title reigns in wrestling history, lasting nearly six years.

Backlund's in-ring style was characterized by technical precision and a relentless work ethic. He was a master of submission holds and grappling techniques, often using the Crossface Chickenwing to secure victories. His matches against legends like Harley Race, Greg Valentine, and Antonio Inoki showcased his versatility and resilience.

One of Backlund's defining moments came in 1983 when he faced Iron Sheik in a match that marked the end of his first title reign. Bob refused to submit, but his manager, Arnold Skaaland, threw in the towel to protect him from injury. This controversial ending paved the way for Hulk Hogan's rise as the next major star, signaling a shift in WWE's direction.

Despite stepping away from wrestling in the mid-1980s, Backlund remained active in the sport. He made a triumphant return to WWE in the 1990s, reinventing himself as a villain. His second WWF Championship win in 1994, defeating Bret Hart in a grueling submission match, proved that Backlund's passion and skill had not waned. His brief reign ended when Diesel defeated him just days later, but his comeback cemented his legacy as a versatile performer.

Backlund faced several challenges throughout his career, including adapting to the evolving wrestling landscape. While the sport shifted towards larger-than-life characters and high-energy entertainment, Backlund stayed true to his disciplined, athletic style. This commitment to authenticity earned him the respect of fans and peers alike.

Outside the ring, Backlund is known for his dedication to fitness and education. He often visited schools and community centers, inspiring young people to pursue their dreams and prioritize discipline. Backlund also published a memoir, Backlund: From All-American Boy to Professional Wrestling's World Champion, which offers an intimate look at his journey and the values that shaped him.

Lesser-known facts about Backlund include his aversion to alcohol and tobacco, his love for reading, and his commitment to helping others. His clean lifestyle and positive outlook made him a role model both in and out of the ring.

Bob Backlund retired from full-time wrestling in the late 1990s but continued to make occasional appearances, reminding fans of his timeless dedication to the sport. His contributions to wrestling earned him a spot in the WWE Hall of Fame in 2013, solidifying his status as one of the greatest champions of all time.

Today, Bob Backlund's legacy endures as a symbol of hard work, integrity, and excellence. His story is a testament to the power of discipline and perseverance, inspiring generations of wrestlers and fans to strive for greatness in every arena of life.

53. Cody Rhodes: The Prince Who Became a King

Cody Garrett Runnels Rhodes, born on June 30, 1985, in Marietta, Georgia, is a professional wrestler known for his charisma, innovation, and resilience. As the son of the legendary Dusty Rhodes, Cody carved out his own path in the wrestling world, transforming from a promising legacy to an industry icon.

Cody grew up in a household where wrestling was more than a profession—it was a way of life. His father, Dusty Rhodes, was one of the most celebrated figures in wrestling, and his half-brother, Dustin Rhodes, also enjoyed a successful career. Despite this legacy, Cody's parents instilled in him the importance of hard work and individuality. As a teenager, Cody excelled in amateur wrestling, winning state championships while attending Lassiter High School in Marietta. He planned to pursue a collegiate wrestling career but decided instead to follow in his father's footsteps. Cody's decision to enter professional wrestling was driven by his admiration for the craft and a desire to honor his family's legacy while building his own.

LEGENDS OF THE WRESTLING RING

Cody began training at Ohio Valley Wrestling (OVW), WWE's developmental territory, in 2006. His natural talent and dedication quickly set him apart. He debuted in OVW as a tag team partner to Shawn Spears, winning the OVW Southern Tag Team Championship. Cody's technical skill, combined with his natural charisma, marked him as a rising star.

In 2007, Cody made his WWE debut on the main roster, initially aligning with Hardcore Holly. The duo captured the World Tag Team Championship, marking Cody's first taste of success on a global stage. However, Cody's career took a major turn when he joined The Legacy, a faction led by Randy Orton that celebrated second-generation wrestlers. This alliance showcased Cody's versatility as both a performer and a character.

Cody's time in WWE saw him adopt various personas, including "Dashing" Cody Rhodes, a vain and self-absorbed character, and a darker, mask-wearing version after suffering a storyline facial injury. These character changes demonstrated his ability to adapt and evolve, keeping his performances fresh and engaging.

Despite his success, Cody felt stifled by the creative limitations in WWE. In 2016, he made the bold decision to leave the company, seeking opportunities on the independent circuit. This move marked a turning point in his career, as Cody began to establish himself as a global wrestling star. He competed in promotions like Ring of Honor (ROH), New Japan Pro-Wrestling (NJPW), and Impact Wrestling, winning championships and earning critical acclaim for his work.

One of Cody's most significant achievements was co-founding All Elite Wrestling (AEW) in 2019 alongside Tony Khan, The Young Bucks, and Kenny Omega. As an executive vice president and in-ring talent, Cody played a pivotal role in shaping AEW into a viable alternative to WWE. His matches, including a memorable bout against Dustin Rhodes at AEW's inaugural Double or Nothing event, highlighted his storytelling ability and emotional depth.

Cody's career has been defined by his ability to overcome challenges and embrace reinvention. From enduring criticism as a "legacy hire" to proving himself as a self-made star, Cody's journey is a testament to perseverance and self-belief. His accomplishments include multiple world championships, the NWA Worlds Heavyweight Championship, and the TNT Championship in AEW.

Lesser-known facts about Cody include his passion for comic books and his love for his dog, Pharaoh, who often accompanied him to the ring. Cody is also a devoted husband to Brandi Rhodes, a fellow wrestler and businesswoman, and a proud father to their daughter, Liberty.

Cody's insights and values reflect his upbringing and experiences. He often speaks about the importance of honoring one's roots while forging a unique path. His decision to return to WWE in 2022 further exemplified his belief in unfinished business and the value of storytelling in wrestling.

Cody Rhodes' story is one of resilience, ambition, and passion. From the shadow of a legendary father to becoming a trailblazer in his own right, Cody has inspired fans and peers alike with his commitment to excellence. As he continues to write his legacy, Cody remains a symbol of what it means to dream big, work hard, and never stop evolving.

54. Roddy Piper: The Rowdy Rebel

Roddy Piper, born Roderick George Toombs on April 17, 1954, in Saskatoon, Saskatchewan, Canada, became one of professional wrestling's most electrifying and controversial figures. Known as "Rowdy" Roddy Piper, he captivated audiences with his unmatched charisma, quick wit, and willingness to push boundaries, solidifying his place as a legend in sports entertainment.

Roddy's early life was marked by struggles. Raised in a modest family, his parents, Eileen and Stanley Toombs, worked hard to make ends meet. His father served as a Royal Canadian Mounted Police officer, a job that required frequent relocations. These moves created challenges for young Roddy, who found himself a target of bullying due to his nomadic lifestyle and Scottish heritage.

At an early age, Roddy turned to combat sports to defend himself and gain confidence. He trained in boxing and amateur wrestling, showcasing natural talent and determination. However, his rebellious nature led him to leave home as a teenager, seeking independence. During this time, he lived in youth hostels and took up odd jobs while pursuing his dream of becoming a professional wrestler.

Roddy entered the wrestling world at the tender age of 15, making his debut in Winnipeg, Manitoba. His first match was a disaster—lasting just seconds—but it fueled his determination to succeed. Roddy adopted the nickname "Rowdy" for his fiery temper and brash attitude, traits that would define his wrestling persona.

In the 1970s, Piper began gaining recognition in regional promotions across North America. His unique gimmick as a bagpipe-playing antagonist with a Scottish heritage quickly set him apart. Piper's ability to rile up crowds with his biting promos and audacious antics made him a sought-after heel (villain).

Roddy's career skyrocketed when he joined the World Wrestling Federation (WWF, now WWE) in 1984. As one of the main villains of the era, he became a key figure in the "Rock 'n' Wrestling" movement, which blended professional wrestling with pop culture. Piper's feud with Hulk Hogan, particularly their clash at the first WrestleMania in 1985, helped catapult WWF into mainstream success.

Piper's talent wasn't limited to wrestling. His talk show segment, "Piper's Pit," became an iconic part of WWF programming. Known for its unscripted chaos, the segment showcased Roddy's sharp wit and ability to create compelling storylines. One memorable moment saw Piper smash a coconut over the head of Jimmy "Superfly" Snuka, cementing his reputation as an unpredictable force.

While Piper often portrayed a villain, his rebellious nature and charisma endeared him to fans, eventually turning him into a beloved anti-hero. Over the course of his career, he won numerous championships, including the WWF Intercontinental Championship and several tag team titles. Despite not holding a world championship, Piper's influence on the industry was immeasurable.

Roddy's career wasn't without challenges. He faced injuries, personal struggles, and the physical toll of wrestling's grueling schedule. Yet, his resilience and love for the business kept him going. Outside the ring, Piper found success in Hollywood, starring in cult classics like

They Live (1988), where his famous line, "I have come here to chew bubblegum and kick ass, and I'm all out of bubblegum," became legendary.

Lesser-known facts about Roddy include his deep love for his family. Despite his wild persona, he was a devoted husband to Kitty and a proud father to four children. He also had a passion for philanthropy, often supporting youth wrestling programs and anti-bullying campaigns.

Roddy Piper passed away on July 31, 2015, at the age of 61 due to a heart attack in Hollywood, California. His death marked the end of an era, but his influence on wrestling and pop culture remains profound.

Roddy Piper's story is one of defiance, resilience, and passion. As "The Rowdy One," he broke barriers and redefined what it meant to be a wrestling star, leaving behind a legacy of unforgettable moments and timeless inspiration.

55. Sting: The Icon of Wrestling

Steve Borden, famously known as Sting, was born on March 20, 1959, in Omaha, Nebraska. As one of the most iconic and enduring figures in professional wrestling, Sting's career is a testament to his resilience, adaptability, and passion for the sport. Known for his enigmatic persona, black-and-white face paint, and signature baseball bat, Sting captivated audiences for decades, transcending eras and promotions.

Sting grew up in a modest household in Southern California after his family relocated from Nebraska. Raised alongside his siblings, he developed a love for sports, particularly basketball and football, during his high school years. Steve's athleticism was evident early on, and he dreamed of becoming a professional athlete. After graduating, he pursued bodybuilding, becoming a regular at Gold's Gym in Venice Beach, California.

While working as a bodybuilder, Steve caught the attention of Rick Bassman, a wrestling promoter. Intrigued by the opportunity, Steve decided to give wrestling a shot, despite having little interest in the sport initially. He trained under Bassman and soon formed a tag team called Power Team USA with fellow trainee Jim Hellwig, who later became The Ultimate Warrior. This marked the beginning of Steve's journey into the world of professional wrestling.

Steve made his wrestling debut in 1985 under the ring name Flash in the Continental Wrestling Association (CWA). However, it was in the Universal Wrestling Federation (UWF) where he began to gain recognition. Rebranding himself as Sting, he adopted a colorful, energetic persona that resonated with fans. Sting's athleticism, charisma, and high-flying maneuvers quickly made him a standout performer.

In 1987, Sting joined Jim Crockett Promotions, which later became World Championship Wrestling (WCW). His rise to stardom was meteoric. Sting's first major moment came at Clash of the Champions I in 1988, where he battled Ric Flair in a 45-minute classic. Although the match ended in a draw, it catapulted Sting into the spotlight, cementing him as a future star.

Throughout the late 1980s and early 1990s, Sting became the face of WCW. He captured his first WCW World Heavyweight Championship in 1990 by defeating Ric Flair at The Great American Bash. Known for his colorful face paint and charismatic energy, Sting was adored by fans of all ages. His rivalries with iconic wrestlers like Vader, The Four Horsemen, and The Great Muta created some of the most memorable moments in wrestling history.

The mid-1990s brought a dramatic shift in Sting's character. As WCW introduced the New World Order (nWo), a villainous faction led by Hulk Hogan, Sting abandoned his vibrant persona for a darker, more mysterious look inspired by the movie The Crow. Dressed in black and white face paint and carrying a baseball bat, Sting became a vigilante figure who fought against the nWo. This transformation revitalized his career and elevated him to legendary status.

Sting's silent, brooding character captivated audiences, and his feud with the nWo became one of the most compelling storylines in wrestling history. At Starrcade 1997, Sting faced Hulk Hogan in a highly anticipated match for the WCW World Heavyweight Championship. Although the match's controversial finish sparked debate, it remains a defining moment in Sting's career.

After WCW's closure in 2001, Sting chose not to join WWE immediately, unlike many of his peers. Instead, he wrestled for Total Nonstop Action Wrestling (TNA) from 2003 to 2014, where he continued to showcase his talent. As a cornerstone of TNA, Sting captured multiple world championships and mentored younger talent, solidifying his legacy as a leader and icon.

Sting's eventual debut in WWE came in 2014, marking a historic moment for fans. He faced Triple H at WrestleMania 31 in 2015 and later challenged Seth Rollins for the WWE World Heavyweight Championship. Unfortunately, a severe neck injury during his match with Rollins forced him into retirement, ending his in-ring career on a bittersweet note.

Lesser-known facts about Sting include his deep Christian faith, which became an essential part of his life in the late 1990s. He credits his faith for helping him overcome personal struggles and maintaining a positive outlook on life. Outside wrestling, Sting is a devoted family man and a passionate advocate for charitable causes.

Sting returned to wrestling in 2020 with All Elite Wrestling (AEW), thrilling fans with his appearances and matches. His resilience and passion for the sport remain as strong as ever, inspiring a new generation of wrestlers and fans.

Sting's journey is a story of reinvention, dedication, and the enduring power of connection. From his colorful beginnings to his iconic transformation, he proved that wrestling is as much about storytelling as it is about athleticism. As "The Icon," Sting's legacy continues to shine brightly in the annals of wrestling history.

***

****

Milton Keynes UK
Ingram Content Group UK Ltd.
UKHW020913291124
451807UK00013B/897